How to Swindle in Chess

Andrew Soltis

Published in the United Kingdom in 2020 by
Batsford, an imprint of
Pavilion Books Company Limited
43 Great Ormond Street
London WC1N 3HZ

ISBN 9781849945639

A CIP catalogue record for this book is available from the
British Library.

25 24 23 22 21 20
10 9 8 7 6 5 4 3 2 1

Printed and bound by CPI Group (UK) Ltd, Croydon CR0 4YY

This book can be ordered direct from the publisher at
www.pavilionbooks.com, or try your local bookshop

Contents

Chapter One:
Outrageous Fortune

Victories show how well you play. Defeats show how unlucky you are.

This is how we often feel when we lose after achieving a promising position: It was an accident. You were on your way to a well-deserved victory. But suddenly something – *something unfair* – spoiled it.

But if luck is random and accidental, why are some players luckier than others?

Anand – Ivanchuk
London 1994

White to play

Black's threats of 23...♗xh1 and 23...♗e3+ must win material. White could have prepared to defend. Instead, he prepared to be lucky, with **23 ♖d3!**.

This stops ...♗e3+ but also threatens to mate with 24 ♖h3 and 25 ♕h8. Experienced players – especially experienced swindlers – try to find moves that not only defend but give them a chance to win.

This was a speed game but Black had time to look at 23...♗xh1. Of course. he saw that on the expected 24 ♖h3 there would be only one good reply, 24...♗e3+!.

That looks strong because 25 ♘d2 allows 25...♕a1 mate and 25 ♔d1 invites a series of powerful checks (25...♕b1+ 26 ♔e2 ♕xc2+ 27 ♔xe3 ♕e4+! 28 ♔d2 ♖fd8+ or 28 ♔f2 ♕f5+ 29 ♔g1 ♕b1+ etc.).

Therefore the normal course of the game was 23...♗xh1 24 ♖h3 ♗e3+ 25 ♖xe3 and the outcome would be highly uncertain.

Instead, Black shot back **23...♖ac8!!**.

White to play

This is stronger than 23...♗xh1 for the same reason White chose 23 ♖d3: It gives him a chance to force a win. If White followed his plan, 24 ♖h3, then 24...♖xc2+! 25 ♔xc2 ♖c8+ hands Black a strong attack.

Black's move did something else, perhaps unintended. It made it much more difficult for either player to calculate accurately. The tactics have become sharper.

That increases the luck factor: White could see how 24 g6 fxg6 25 ♘xg6 threatens 26 ♘e7 mate.

But only if he had plenty of time could he foresee what might happen after 25...♖xc2+ 26 ♔xc2 ♖c8+. (A perpetual check is likely: 27 ♔d1 ♕b1+ 28 ♔e2 ♗xh1 29 ♘e7+.)

Instead, luck intruded. He played **24 ♖h3?** and the position became chaotic, **24...♖xc2+! 25 ♔xc2 ♖c8+.** As the players got closer to forfeiting on time, the luck factor was soaring.

White to play

White could safeguard his king with 26 ♖c3!. But that gives up hope of ♕h8 mate. The initiative would be Black's and he would have all the winning chances after 26...♗e4+!.

White went for broke with **26 ♔d1??** and kept his ♕h8 mate plan alive.

After **26...♕b1+! 27 ♔e2** he would win in case of 27...♕c2+?? 28 ♘d2!.

Then Black would only have a few checks left, such as 28...♗f3+ 29 ♔xf3! ♕f5+. He could safely resign following 30 ♔g2.

But only when the game is over can you be sure about tactical shots like these. That is when you know which player was the lucky one. Or, rather, the luckier one.

Black to play

With **27...♕e4+!** it seemed certain that Black was the luckier. He could now force checkmate in, at most, five moves.

It would be faster after 28 ♔d1 ♕c2 mate and 28 ♔f1 ♕e1 mate.

White kept the game going with **28 ♔xf2 ♖c2+ 29 ♔f1**. The game should have ended with 29...♕xh1 mate.

Had that happened, White could have honestly said it was an unfair result. After all, he had found a great move in 23 ♖d3!, when it seemed his only options were dismal – such as 23 ♕e2? ♗xh1 that only prolong a losing game.

Besides that, he would probably have drawn if he had had the time to calculate 24 g6!.

But he didn't have to complain about bad luck that day.

Black to play

Incredibly, Black overlooked 29...♕xh1 mate. He played **29...♕f4+???**.

This should have turned certain victory into probable defeat following **30 ♘f3!**. White had renewed the threat of 31 ♕h8 mate, while holding an extra rook and a piece. Black would run out of checks soon after 30...♖c1+ 31 ♘xc1 ♕xc1+ 32 ♔g2.

But White only had slightly more time than Black. After **30...♔f8** he passed up the routine and easily winning 31 ♕h8+ and 32 ♕xg7.

Instead, this strange game continued strangely, **31 g6?? ♕c4+ 32 ♔g1 ♕xb3 33 ♕e5 ♖c1+ 34 ♔f2 ♕c2+ 35 ♔e3 ♕b3+ 36 ♔e2? ♕c4+?** (36...♗xf3+) **37 ♔f2 ♕c2+ 38 ♔e3 ♕b3+!**.

White to play

White avoided perpetual check with **39 ♔f4??**. He was lost, **39...♖c4+! 40 ♘d4 ♕xh3 41 ♕b8+ ♖c8 42 ♕d6+**.

But as Black played **42...♔g8!** his flag fell. And these were two of the very best players in the world.

One-player luck

What can we make of this? Clearly, the outcome was extremely lucky. That is, unexpected. But was it just horribly played by both players?

To say that we have to look only at the ghastly moves and ignore the splendid ones (23 ♖d3!, 23...♖ac8!!, 24...♖xc2+!, 27...♕e4+!, 30 ♘f3!, 38...♕b3+!, 39...♖c4+!).

White played more of the bad moves and Black found more of the good ones. But they both chose to increase the likelihood of a lucky result. Both players wanted to be the lucky one.

As much as we ascribe success in chess to other factors, luck abounds. It happens at the amateur level and among super-GMs. "We have a lucky champion," Vladimir Kramnik said when then-world champion Garry Kasparov had once again escaped from a bad position against him.

Yuri Averbakh was a promising scientist when he considered switching careers and becoming a professional chessplayer. A friend who was a strong master told him he was "out of his mind." It is crazy to get into a line of work, the friend said, "where so much depends on luck."

Lucky results are by nature unfair, sometimes outrageously so. A player who did nothing but try to avoid losing gets a full point. His opponent commits suicide. We can call these cases of one-player luck:

Bu – Nakamura
Gibraltar 2008

White to play

Black had constructed an impregnable fortress earlier. White's queen cannot win unassisted. He managed to send his king on a voyage from c5 to a7, then c8 and d8, and finally c7. But there was no progress to be made.

Yet there was a decisive result. White played **68 ♔d6??** and permitted **68...♘e4 mate.**

Black was lucky. But the finish wasn't a true swindle. Black resisted. But he did nothing to provoke 68 ♔d6.

A swindle is something else. The would-be swindler chooses moves that do more than just resist. He defends actively, often by setting traps. The more primitive the trap, the more an unexpected result seems lucky. Here's an example from the very first international tournament.

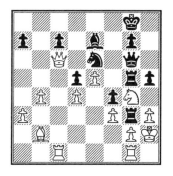

Staunton – Anderssen
London 1851

White to play

Black is winning. The white knight is attacked and pinned because 29 ♘f2 loses to 29...♖xg2+.

White could try 29 ♕xd5 hxg4 30 hxg4, thinking he would have two pawns as compensation for the knight.

But that allows an immediate mate by a queen check at h6 or h7.

Only slightly better is 30 fxg4 in view of 30...♖5xg4! (since 31 hxg4 allows another mating queen check).

White played the desperate **29 ♘f6+!**.

It was confusing to Black, if only because he had six legal responses.

Black to play

The first was the most natural, 29...gxf6. But after 30 ♕xe6+ Black's win is gone:

White can take the bishop with check after 30...♔h7? or 30...♔g7?.

He can meet 30...♔h8 with 31 ♕xe7 because 31...♖xg2+ 32 ♖xg2 ♖xg2+ 33 ♔h1 ends Black's mating attack.

Then Black has to find 33...♖h2+! 34 ♔xh2 ♕g3+ to draw by perpetual check.

There was more for Black to look at. He must have seen that he could meet 29 ♘f6+ with 29...♔h8.

But once again he would have nothing much after 30 ♕xe6 ♖xg2+ 31 ♖xg2 ♖xg2+ 32 ♔h1 or just 30 ♕e8+ ♕xe8 31 ♘xe8.

So, Black played the only move that discouraged ♕xe6. The game ended with **29...♔f7?? 30 ♕e8 mate.**

That swindle required the efforts of both players. It was, of course, an unfair result. Black could have won with 29...♗xf6! 30 ♕xe6+ ♔h7! because of 31 exf6 ♖xg2+ 32 ♖xg2 ♖xg2+ 33 ♔h1 ♕g3!.

Nevertheless, 29 ♘f6+ was the pragmatic move because it had the greatest chance of saving the game.

Practical versus "computer-best"

Chess has gotten a lot more sophisticated since 1851. We defend much better today. But we are also much better at swindling.

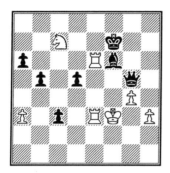

Topalov – Glavina
San Cugat 1992

White to play

White has barely survived since he blundered away his queen earlier. Black's last move, 49...c3, prepared to queen a pawn and end resistance.

A passive defense such as 50 ♖e2 would lose in various ways. One is 50...d4 and ...d3. Another is 50...c2 51 ♖xc2 ♗e5 followed by either 52...♕f4+ or 52...♗xc7 53 ♖xc7+ ♔xe6.

White kept hope alive with **50 ♘e8!**, attacking the f6-bishop.

It is not just the move with the best chance of avoiding a loss. It is the move with the best chance of winning: 50...♗d4?? 51 ♘d6+ ♔g8 52 ♖e8+ ♔h7 53 ♖2e7+.

Then 53...♔h6 54 ♘f7+ or 53...♗g7 54 ♖h8+! ♔xh8 55 ♘f7+.

Only slightly better is 50...♗d8? in view of 51 ♘d6+ ♔g8 52 ♘f5 c2 53 ♖c6 and White has turned the game around.

But he was lost after **50...c2!**.

White to play

White's 50 ♘e8! was objectively the best move available. The swindle begins now: The "computer-best" move – the one recommended by engines – is a bad choice.

Computers recommend 51 ♖xf6+. Black has nothing better than 51...♕xf6 52 ♘xf6 c1(♕) with a long ♕-vs-♖+♘ endgame ahead.

White might draw if he could play 53 ♘xd5. But that loses to 53...♕h1+ and ...♕xd5.

So he would have to play another knight move and try to defend after, say, 53...d4. Computers say White might hold on for 30 moves before he gets mated.

But White realized he had greater practical chances with **51 ♘xf6**. Then 51...♕xf6?? loses because 52 ♖xf6 is check and White has time for 53 ♖c3.

So play went **51...c1(♕)! 52 ♖e7+.**

Black to play

This is a true swindle attempt because:

(a) With proper play, Black would win more quickly than if White had played the computer-best 51 ♖xf6+, and

(b) White is setting traps. So far they are simple ones – 52...♔xf6?? 53 ♖3e6 mate and 52...♔f8?? 53 ♘h7+.

Black is playing well and **52...♔g6!** should have won. White had one trick left, **53 ♘h5!**. It threatened to win with 54 ♖3e6+.

It is surprising to see that even with two queens, Black would achieve nothing from checks (53...♕h1+ 54 ♔g3 ♕g1+ 55 ♔f3 ♕d1+ 56 ♔g3).

But when you have two queens you have the luxury of giving one away: **53...♕xe7! 54 ♖xe7 ♕xa3+ 55 ♖e3 ♕a1**.

White to play

This ♕-vs.-♖+♘ ending is much easier to win than the one that might have arisen after 51 ♖xf6+ ♕xf6. Black doesn't have to create a passed queenside pawn now. They already exist. He can just push one to the eighth rank.

White can do little to stop that. He would lose soon after 56 ♘f4+ ♔f7 57 ♘xd5? ♕h1+ and ...♕xd5.

A better try is 57 g5 and 58 g6+. This looked dangerous. Looks help create swindles.

But this look is a bluff. After 57...b4 58 g6+ ♔f8 White can safely resign (59 ♘e6+ ♔g8 or 59 h4 b3 60 ♖xb3? ♕d1+).

But Black correctly saw that on **56 ♘f4+** he can restrain the white pawns with **56...♔g5** and also threaten to win the knight (57...♕f1+!).

If White safeguarded the knight with 57 ♘e2, Black wins by pushing (57...b4 or 57...a5 and 58...a4).

So White defended against ...♕f1+ with **57 ♔g3** and then **57...♕g1+!** **58 ♘g2**.

Black to play

White's knight has become a pinned, inactive piece. Black had no reason to fear 59 ♖e5+ ♔g6 60 ♖xd5 because his remaining pawns are too strong (60...b4).

13

He must have noticed that 59 h4+ was possible. But the king could safely retreat to f6 or g6.

Since there was apparently no threat, Black played **58...a5??**.

But he resigned after **59 ♖e6!**. There was no way to stop 60 h4 mate.

Championship Swindling

Why do some great players become world champion and others don't? Paul Keres – one of those in the "don't" category – had an answer: Champions are lucky. The others aren't.

Keres cited the 1959 Candidates tournament. He scored an impressive three wins out of four games against Mikhail Tal. But Tal won the tournament and became world champion the next year.

Keres particularly remembered one game, which Tal drew from a dead lost position. 'You cannot fight against such luck," Keres told fellow GM Bent Larsen. Games like that convinced Keres that "fate was against him," Larsen recalled.

Tal's luck, like that of all great swindlers, was a collaboration. But it was not a collaboration of him and some mysterious force of destiny. It required the unintended cooperation by his opponent, who had been world champion just one year before.

Smyslov – Tal
Candidates tournament 1959

1 e4 c5 2 ♘f3 e6 3 d4 cxd4 4 ♘xd4 a6 5 ♗d3 ♘c6 6 ♘xc6 bxc6 7 0-0 d5 8 ♘d2 ♘f6 9 ♕e2 ♗e7 10 ♖e1 0-0 11 b3 a5 12 ♗b2 a4 13 a3 axb3 14 cxb3 ♕b6 15 exd5 cxd5 16 b4 ♘d7 17 ♘b3 e5 18 ♗f5 e4 19 ♖ec1 ♕d6 20 ♘d4 ♗f6 21 ♖c6 ♕e7 22 ♖ac1 h6 23 ♖c7! ♗e5 24 ♘c6!

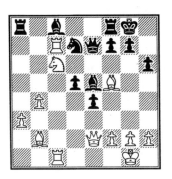

Black to play

Tal would lose material if his attacked queen goes to e8 (25 ♘xe5 ♘xe5 26 ♖xc8).

14

The computer-best 24...♕f6 would also lose after 25 ♗xe5 ♘xe5 26 ♘e7+ and ♗xc8.

Moreover, Tal had spent so much time trying to conjure up counterplay earlier that he only had two or three minutes to reach the time control at move 40.

"I had nothing to lose," Tal admitted afterward. "I attempted only to complicate my opponent's task in any way possible."

He seized his slim chance for kingside play with **24...♕g5**.

This could lose faster than 24...♕f6. The reason is **25 h4!** since 25...♕xf5?? 26 ♘e7+ hangs the queen.

So play went **25...♕xh4 26 ♘xe5 ♘xe5 27 ♖xc8**.

Black to play

White has won a piece for a pawn. Computers will tell you Black's best options are 27...♘d3 and 27...♕f4. But they admit that those moves offer almost no survival chances after 28 ♖xa8 ♖xa8 29 ♖c8+ ♖xc8 30 ♗xc8.

Tal's instinct told him to search for tactics, any tactics that offered hope. He found **27...♘f3+ 28 gxf3 ♕g5+**.

Then 29 ♗g4 ♖fxc8 wins back material and 29 ♔h1 ♕h5+ 30 ♔g1 ♕g5+ repeats the position.

White was playing the best moves and that continued **29 ♔f1! ♕xf5 30 ♖xf8+ ♖xf8 31 fxe4 dxe4**.

Tal was not playing "best" moves and that is why White's advantage has grown substantially since 24...♕g5. His opponent assumed Tal was playing badly because he now had only seconds left.

White to play

But Tal had created tactical opportunities on White's weakened light squares that White's extra piece – a dark-squared bishop – cannot deal easily with.

Instead, White can use his heavy pieces to defend the kingside. Both 32 ♖c3 or 32 ♕e3 are useful.

White preferred **32 ♕e3** so his queen could go to g3, where it would threaten ♕xg7 mate. That threat would either prompt a losing queen trade (...♕g5) or a weakening of Black's own kingside (...f6 or ...g5).

Computers say Tal's **32...♖d8** made matters even worse for him. But for the first time in several moves he was making a real threat (33...♖d3! 34 ♕c5 ♕h3+ or 34 ♕e2 e3).

White answered with the move he had planned, **33 ♕g3**, so that 33...f6? 34 ♖c7.

Tal replied **33...g5**

White to play

This is the first point in the game when we can say White erred. With 34 ♕c3! f6 35 ♕b3+! he would edge closer to victory.

For example, 35...♔g7 36 ♖c7+ ♔g6? 37 ♕f7 is mate. On 35...♔h8 he has 36 ♖c6 followed by a capture on f6 or even 36 ♖c5! ♕f4 37 ♖c6!.

But when you have as great an advantage as White, you don't feel that a lot of calculating is necessary. Vasily Smyslov saw something that looked simpler and stronger, **34 ♖c5**.

Then 34...♕e6 allows 35 ♖xg5+! (35...hxg5 36 ♕xg5+ ♕g6 37 ♕xd8+).

Tal used his best tactical resource, **34...♖d1+**. Once again, White avoided calculating long lines (like 35 ♔e2 ♕d7 36 ♕b8+). He chose the more natural **35 ♔g2** and after **35...♕e6**:

White to play

Black is threatening ...nothing. But he keeps creating situations in which his opponent has not-so-simple choices.

Here it looks like there must be a forced mate after 36 ♕b8+ ♔h7 37 ♕h8+ ♔g6 38 ♕g8+ ♔h5. But there is no mate, just an eventual win after 39 ♕c8!.

Rather than calculate lines like that, White assumed he could win with his pawns, **36 b5**.

Then **36...♔h7!** eliminated a check with ♕b8. That doesn't seem like much – until you see that Black now has a threat, 37...♖d3!.

For example, 38 ♕e5 ♕h3+ and mates, or 38 ♕h2 ♕g4+.

Both players were now short of time and four moves away from the time control. The natural moves **37 ♖c6 ♕d5** were played.

White to play

This is the position that convinced fans – and Paul Keres – of Tal's luck.

17

It looks like the best position White has had all game. And it is: He can win outright with 38 ♕h2! because of the threat of 39 ♕xh6+ and mates.

But to play 38 ♕h2! White had to see that 38...e3+ could be safely met by 39 ♔g3!. Black would almost certainly have resigned then.

But what happened was **38 ♕e5?? ♖g1+!.** White may have seen 39 ♔xg1 ♕d1+ 40 ♔g2 ♕g4+ 41 ♔g3 but not 40...♕f3+! 41 ♔h2 ♕h5+ with perpetual check.

The game ended with **39 ♔h2 ♖h1+! 40 ♔g1 ♖g1+ draw.** Tal was told after the game that Smyslov had seen 38...♖g1+ but not 39...♖h1+.

It is easy to explain the surprise finish by saying that White missed a tactic. But it took a remarkable effort for Tal to have *any* tactics after 24 ♘c6!. The final result depended on White's contribution – and Black's.

The first time that Pal Benko, another world-class player of that day, played Tal he had a winning position after 39 moves. Then he made three bad moves in a row. He awarded himself a total of five question marks for them. He lost and said it was his first experience with "the legendary Tal luck." As usual with a swindle victim, he didn't appreciate what his opponent did to create that luck.

Next-to-Last

Luck is fickle. It can help one player and then switch affections to the other.

That is what happened at the end of the Smyslov – Tal game. But no one appreciated it at the time.

Black to play

Black's **37...♕d5??** was actually a blunder.

Correct was 37...♕f5! with at least a draw because of the threat of 38...♖d3.

Then 38 ♕e5?? allows 38...♕f3+ and mate next. And 38 ♖c3 ♕xb5 threatens 38...♕f1+ as well as 38...♕xb2.

So Tal was lucky that Smyslov answered 37...♕d5?? with **38 ♕e5??**. But if Smyslov had found 38 ♕h2!, fans would say he was the lucky one, because Tal missed 37...♕f5!.

Savielly Tartakower made many wise observations but perhaps the one that is most useful to a competitive player is:

The winner is the player who makes the next-to-last error.

This is an exaggeration but with Tarkakover's usual kernel of truth: One mistake rarely decides a game. What is typical is a series of mutual errors. This is what a would-be swindler has to expect – and exploit.

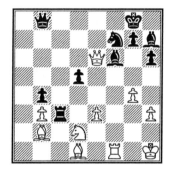

Goletiani – Sharevich
St. Louis 2015

White to play

The position is so highly double-edged that any mistake is bound to swing the advantage to one side. In mutual time pressure, mistakes – plural – are likely.

For example, 36 ♗xc3 is obvious. But it turns out badly after 36...bxc3. If the attacked knight moves it allows 37 ...♗e4!, e.g. 37 ♘f3 ♗e4! and ...♕g3! (38 ♔g2 ♗h4).

White found **36 ♗f3!** with a threat to win with 37 ♗xd5.

Black needed more than a routine reply. She would face a very hard defense after 36...♕c8? 37 ♕xc8+ ♖xc8 38 ♗xf6 and ♗xd5.

After the game, 36...♔h8! was discovered. Then Black threatens to win with 37...♘g5 (38 ♕xd5 ♖d3). And 37 ♕xf7 ♖c7 is fine (38 ♕-moves ♗xb2).

But she played **36...♖c2??**.

White to play

That was the first twist of fate. It seemed that 37 ♗xf6 would lose to 37...♖xd2 followed by 38...♕h2 mate or 38...gxf6.

But what both players overlooked was that 37 ♗xf6 ♖xd2 allows a winning 38 ♗e5! (38...♕xe5 39 ♕c8+ and mates).

If the game had ended with that mate, or after 38...♕d8 39 ♗d4! and 40 ♗xd5, we would know what the final mistake of the game was.

But the effects of 36...♖c2?? were reversed by **37 ♗xd5??**.

Why would this seem like the right move? Because it was more forcing than 37 ♗xf6. It threatens mate after 38 ♕xf7+ and 39 ♗xf6. And it wins after 37...♖xb2 38 ♕xf7+ and 39 ♖xf6!.

But Black could have turned a lost position into a winning one with 37...♖xd2!.

That threatens mate on h2. This time 38 ♕xf7+ ♔h8 39 ♗e5 fails to 39...♗xe5 40 ♕f8+ ♗g8!.

Instead, the wheel of fortune was turned again by **37...♗g6??** and then **38 ♗xf6 ♖xd2 39 ♗e5!**.

Black to play

20

This time White saw this move. It works, but not nearly as well in the 37 ♗xf6 ♖xd2 38 ♗e5! version.

Black faced another crucial decision. Both 39...♕d8 and 39...♕b5 would threaten ...♕xd5+.

In either case, 40 ♖xf7 ♕xd5+ 41 ♕xd5 ♖xd5 42 ♖xg7+ would grant White a very good endgame.

But that is the best Black can get now. There was no better 39th move for Black.

In time pressure it is natural to play the most forceful move. Here 39...♕b5 seems better than 39 ...♕d8 because it also threatens 40...♕f1+. It would virtually force White to respond 40 ♖xf7.

But Black chose **39...♕d8!**.

White to play

A good swindler knows that often the less forcing move has greater chance of inducing an error because it gives the opponent more choice.

White might consider 40 ♗g2 because it threatens to win quickly with ♕xg6. There is even a pretty mate, 40...♔h7? 41 ♕xg6+! ♔xg6 42 ♗e4+ and so on.

But Black would meet 40 ♗g2? with 40...♕d7. Then the 41 ♕xd7 ♖xd7 endgame is a bit less disadvantageous than the one that would arise after 39...♕b5 40 ♖xf7 ♕xd5+.

Black reaped an unexpected bonus when White passed up both 40 ♖xf7! and 40 ♗g2? in favor of **40 e4??**.

Once again, a logical move is a blunder. After **40...♕h4!** White was getting mated.

So which move was decisive?

It wasn't 36...♖c2??, because White responded with 37 ♗xd5??.

It wasn't 37...♗g6?? because the outcome was still in some doubt.

No, only the last blunder, 40 e4??, would be called unlucky.

Chess can be a game of swift and fatal changes. Positions are turned from losing to winning in a move or two. You can deplore the changes as unfair. They often are. But if you want to live in the real world of chess luck you need to take advantage of it. That is what this book is about.

Quiz

There will be quiz positions at the end of each chapter. Solutions on pages 235-240.

1.

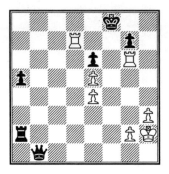

**Le Quang Liem –
Caruana**
St. Louis 2017

White to play

White should lose regardless of how he captures on g7. Why did he pick **50 ♖dxg7** ?

2.

Jakovenko – Grischuk
Khanty-Mansiysk 2009

Black to play

The final moves were **56...♖a1 57 ♔d2 ♖a2+ 58 ♔d1 ♖f2 59 ♗d2 ♖f5 60 ♗e1 ♖d5 61 ♔d2 ♖d4 62 ♖g3+ ♔f1 63 ♔e3 ♖d5 64 ♗f2 resigns**.

How many of these moves were blunders?

3.

Nakamura – Carlsen
St. Louis 2017

White to play

And which, if any, of these moves were blunders? – **88 ♔b1 ♖d2 89 ♗xg1 ♖d1+ 90 ♔b2 e1(♕) 91 ♖xe1 ♖xe1 92 ♗b6 draw**.

Chapter Two:
Swindle-Think

Frank Marshall didn't invent swindling. But he made it his trademark, even naming the first collection of his games "Marshall's Chess Swindles."

What Marshall appreciated better than his contemporaries is that in bad positions there are fundamentally different criteria for choosing moves. The standards that we usually trust to point us towards the most successful moves often do not apply.

Marshall – Gruenfeld
Moscow 1925

1 e4 e5 2 ♘f3 ♘c6 3 ♘c3 ♘f6 4 ♗b5 ♘d4 5 ♗c4 ♗c5 6 d3 d6 7 ♘a4 ♗b6 8 ♘xb6 ♘xf3+ 9 gxf3!? axb6 10 ♖g1 0-0 11 ♗g5 ♗e6 12 ♕d2 ♔h8 13 ♗h4?

Black to play

Marshall has been seeking play on the g-file since 9 gxf3. His last move prepares a typical Marshall sacrifice, 14 0-0-0 followed by 15 ♖xg7! ♔xg7 15 ♕g5+ ♔h8 16 ♕xf6+ and mates.

But he overlooked **13...♘xe4!**. It is based on 14 ♗xd8 ♘xd2, when Black emerges with an extra pawn or more (15 ♔xd2 ♖fxd8 or 15 ♗xc7? ♘xf3+).

If he was looking to minimize Black's advantage Marshall would have found 14 ♕h6!, the "computer-best" move and also a clever one. It damages Black's pawn structure by forcing 14...gxh6, so that 15 ♗xd8 ♖fxd8 16 fxe4 gives him a fighting chance in the endgame.

Marshall wasn't interested in hours of dogged and perhaps doomed defense. He raised the ante with a second pawn, **14 fxe4? ♕xh4 15 ♕c3 ♕xh2**.

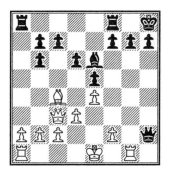

White to play

Nor was he inclined to the computer-best 15 ♕g5 ♕xg5 16 ♖xg5.

He chose **16 0-0-0** and then came **16...♗xc4 17 ♕xc4.**

Black could have safely grabbed a third pawn (17...♕xf2). But two pawns is enough to win any foreseeable endgame – and an endgame seemed to be coming soon, thanks to his next moves, **17...♕h6+ 18 ♔b1 ♕e6!.**

But there was no way Marshall was going to accommodate him with 19 ♕xe6?. He has been seeing things differently since move 14.

White to play

He stopped trying to just minimize Black's advantage, the way a computer would. Instead, he began thinking like a swindler.

He looked for tactical chances. But after **19 ♕xc7** it seemed clear that Black had all the possible checks and dangerous moves, beginning with **19...♕xa2+ 20 ♔c1.**

Marshall understood that when a player has the kind of material advantage that Black enjoys here, he is not likely to look for sacrifices. (The game might have been over before move 30 if Black had found 20...♖fc8 21 ♕xb6 ♖c6 22 ♕xb7 ♖cc8! and ...♖cb8.)

Much more likely is what happened, **20...♕a1+ 21 ♔d2.**

25

Black to play

Believe it or not, this is the kind of position Marshall had been seeking since 14 fxe4. For the first time since then he has tactical chances.

For example, 21...♕a5+ 22 ♔e2! would tempt Black to take another pawn, 22...♖ac8 23 ♕e7 ♖xc2+.

But after 24 ♔f3 there are no more checks and Black's f8-rook is hanging. He would be mated after 24...♔g8? 25 ♖xg7+! ♔xg7 26 ♖g1+.

The same ♖xg7! tactic works after 24...♕a8 25 ♖xg7! when Black has to try for a draw with 25...♕d8!.

Even the apparent safety-move, 24...♖g8, only draws after 25 ♖xg7!. For example, 25...♖xg7! 26 ♕d8+ ♖g8 27 ♕f6+ ♖g7 28 ♕d8+.

Black may or may not have seen all this. But after **21...♕xb2** he was shocked by – you guessed it – **22 ♖xg7!** one more time.

Black to play

This time 22...♔xg7? loses, to 23 ♖g1+ and 24 ♕e7!.

It is too late to offer a queen trade, 22...♕b4+ 23 ♔e2 ♕c5, because 24 ♕e7 assures a draw.

But you can bet that Marshall would have played 24 ♖h1! instead. It threatens 25 ♖hxh7 mate. It's the best move because it requires Black to find a defense that is not so obvious, 24...♚xg7 25 ♕e7! h6!. Then 26 ♖g1+ ♚h7 27 ♕f6 draws.

In any case, Black played the move that looked crushing, **22...♖ac8**.

Then the star move in other variations, 23 ♕e7, loses to 23...♖xc2+ 24 ♚e1 ♖e2+ 25 ♖f2+ 26 ♚g1 ♚xg7.

But Marshall had perpetual check with **23 ♖xh7+! ♚xh7 24 ♖h1+**. The rest was **24...♚g6 25 ♖g1+ ♚h6 26 ♖h1+ ♚g6 27 ♖g1+ draw**.

If the king tries to advance to f4 it allows a deadly queen check (25...♚h5 26 ♖h1+ ♚g4?? 27 ♕d7+! or 25...♚h6 26 ♖h1+ ♚g5?? 27 ♕e7+).

Black's final mistake was 21...♕xb2. What was his first? Ironically, it was the cautious 17...♕h6+/18...♕e6 – and the assumption that White would play his "best" available moves.

Computers confirm that 19 ♕c7! was not just a crazy Marshall move. It was the best move available.

And, as often happens in a great swindle, there were less detectable mistakes. Black could have won with 21...♕a5+ 22 ♚e2 ♕c5.

Computer versus Coffeehouse

Today we regard computers as the ultimate chess authorities. We check our opinion of the move we want to play with an engine's evaluation. We feel good when our choice is rated number one by the machine. If our move isn't rated the best, we try to figure out why not.

But often the move most likely to succeed against a human is not the move a computer strongly recommends. One game in particular made this difference known.

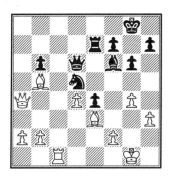

Duchess – Kaissa
World Computer
Championship 1977

White to play

In a battle of two of the strongest engines of the day, White played **34 ♕a8+**. Black replied **34...♖e8** and lost, of course, following **35 ♕xe8+**.

The spectators – who included former world champion Mikhail Botvinnik – were stunned. Botvinnik helped create Kaissa. Why, he wondered, did it put a rook en prise? Obviously, 34...♔g7 was the right move, wasn't it?

No, it was the second worst move (after 34...♕d8??). The reason is that White could have answered 34...♔g7 with 35 ♕f8+! ♔xf8 36 ♗h6+ and mate with ♖c8+.

In contrast, 34...♖e8 prolonged the game. It lasted until move 48 when it was adjudicated a win for White.

This is the problem that players face in the 21st century when they get a bad position. If they think like computers and play the "computer-best" moves they will last longer – provided they are playing computers.

But if their opponent is a human, they should think differently. Against a human, the only move to consider is 34...♔g7. A fallible White might not see 35 ♕f8+. Both moves *should* lose. But one offers a chance not to.

Least Worst

Computers don't see the significance of that difference. Their algorithms are calibrated to find the least-worst move in a lost position. A move that keeps a Black disadvantage at +5.00 – the equivalent of an extra rook – must be better than one that allows a disadvantage of +6.00. Computers like *minimizing* moves.

Good swindlers see no benefit in minimizing. Rather than endure a hopeless position an additional ten, twenty or thirty moves, they will go for the move that offers some hope.

Jimenez – Larsen
Palma de Mallorca 1971

Black to play

White has enough of a material edge to win, a queen and a pawn in return for a rook and bishop. Computers say Black should be passive, even if it surrenders the e-pawn.

For example, 31...♔h7 and 32 ♕xe5 ♖e7 is rated as Black's best by some programs. They place White's advantage at about +3.00.

But computers don't take into account how easy a "won position" is for a human to win. In this case, it would be fairly easy – 33 ♕f4 followed by 34 h3, 35 ♔h2 and eventually g2-g4.

Instead, Black chose **31...♗c6!**. It set a trap, 32 ♕xe5? ♖e7 33 ♕b8+ ♖e8 34 ♕-moves ♖e1+.

Why do computers reject it? The reason is 32 ♖d2!. It makes 33 ♕xe5 possible under better conditions than after 31...♔h7 since White can use his rook in key continuations.

The best answer to 32 ♖d2! is 32...e4 but then 33 ♖d6! runs Black out of useful moves.

Black to play

He would be mated after 33...♖h7 34 ♖d8+ ♔g7 35 ♕e5+, for example.

Another mate arrives after 33...f4 34 ♖d8+ ♔h7 35 ♕h3+! ♔g6 36 ♕g4+ ♔h6 37 ♕h4+ ♔g6 38 ♖d6+.

Black could hold his disadvantage to about +4.00 with 33...♔h7 34 ♕h6+ ♔g8 35 ♖d8+ ♖f8 36 ♕e6+ ♖f7 37 ♕g6+ ♖g7 38 ♖xf8+ ♔xf8 39 ♕xf5+.

If the computer could talk it would say, "Don't you know that +3.00 is less than +4.00? Therefore, 31...♔h7 was the least-worst move."

But a human says: "If I am lost in any case, I should play 31...♗c6. White may find a not-so-obvious move – 33 ♖d6! – to beat me. If he doesn't, my chances are a lot better than after 31...♔h7." And that is the right way to think...if you are a human.

White played a good move instead, making *luft* for his king with **32 h4**.

Black to play

Minimizing often means defeatism. Some computers recommend the doomed policy of 32...♔h7. They have nothing good to suggest after 33 ♕xe5.

But Black correctly played **32...e4**. Why correct? Because it is the only move with realistic chances of survival. And it sets another trap, 33 ♖xf5?? ♗d7!.

Objectively, Black is getting closer to defeat. He would be mated soon after 33 ♖d2! f4? 34 ♖d8+ ♔h7 35 ♕e5!, for instance (36 ♕h5).

But White would have to calculate his way through lines such as 33...♔h7 34 ♖d6 ♗d7 35 ♕d5 ♗c6 36 ♕e5 or 35 ♕e5 ♖e7 36 ♕d5 when his progress is evident only to an engine.

So, after repeating the position, **33 ♕c8+ ♖f8 34 ♕e6+ ♖ff7**, White tried **35 h5**.

He was still winning after **35...♗d7 36 ♕e5 ♖e7 37 ♕b8+ ♔h7**. But the immediate crisis had eased. Black was not losing one of his central pawns as it seemed before 31...♗c6..

White to play

Moreover, Black's pawns had become weapons (38 ♕xb7 e3! 39 ♖e2 ♗b5 or 39 ♖f1 ♗b5).

After some minor slips, Black managed to draw **38 ♕f4 e3 39 ♖e2 ♖e4 40 ♕d6 ♗e6 41 b3 ♖d7 42 ♕g3 ♖d1+ 43 ♔h2 ♖g4 44 ♕e5? ♖h4+** (45 ♔g3 ♖g4+ 46 ♔f3? ♗d5+).

Of course, most positions as lost as Black's in the first diagram cannot be saved. Near-miracles don't happen every day.

But playing computer-best moves, such as 31...♔h7, offered virtually no chance at all. You have to give yourself a chance to become lucky.

A New Symbol

Chess annotation has had certain conventions for well over a century. Among the oldest are awarding an exclamation point to a good move and a question mark to a bad one.

But we don't have a good way of denoting a move that is objectively second-best – or third-best or fourth-best – yet is the most *practical*.

For the rest of this book we will use a new symbol – ~ – to denote such a move. In the Duchess – Kaissa game, 34...♔g7 objectively deserves a question mark. After all, it allows immediate checkmate.

But to appreciate it, we should make it **34...♔g7~**.

The same goes for Bent Larsen's **30...♗c6~** and **31...e4~** in the game that followed.

The basic principle of Swindle-Think is this:

In lost positions, forget about finding the objectively "best" move. Look instead for the one most likely to succeed against a human.

Knowing that your position cannot be saved through normal means should free you to think differently.

Fischer – Reshevsky
Herceg-Novi 1970

White to play

Black's last move, ...d3, unleashed a decisive attack on the white queen (30...♗xa1).

There is no defense because of 31 ♖bb2 ♗xb2 32 ♕xb2 a1(♕), for example.

The only difficult variation to calculate was 32 ♖xb2 d2! 33 ♖xd2 ♕b1 and now 34 ♖d1 ♕xd1! allows the a-pawn to queen.

Bobby Fischer called **30 ♖xa2** "a last swindle try." It's a true swindle because it can be refuted in a way that would enlarge Black's advantage – 30...♖xa2 31 ♕xa2 ♕xe1+ 32 ♔g2 d2. After he queens he will emerge at least a bishop ahead.

Yet Black fell for **30...♗xa1??** and turned a big material plus into a minus after **31 ♖xa8+ ♔g7 32 ♖xa1**.

White coordinated his pieces, stopped the black d-pawn and soon won it, **32...d2 33 ♘g2 ♕xd5 34 ♖bb1 b5 35 ♖d1 b4 36 ♘e3 ♕d3 37 ♘f1**. Black soon resigned.

Computers would punctuate the key moves as 31 ♖bb2! and 31 ♖xa2? but a swindler knows it should be **31 ♖bb2?** and **31 ♖xa2~**.

Swindling versus Gambling

Many players believe chess is a sport. But there is a fundamental difference when it comes to decision making.

In sports, a risky decision is typically judged by its result. The tennis player who rushes the net, the hockey coach who pulls his goalie, the gymnast who tries a particularly difficult routine: They are called brilliant if they succeed. They are judged foolhardy if they don't.

Chess is different. We know that bad moves can win games. They win when they encourage a bad response. As Tartakower indicated, the blunder that counts is the last one.

A swindle attempt is judged by other criteria, including by how bad the alternatives are. If there are valid alternatives, a risky move may be just an unjustified throw of the dice.

Shabalov – Benjamin
Long Beach 1993

White to play

In this tense game from a US Championship White had just thrown away a big advantage and, à la Tartakower, Black returned the favor.

Play went **35 e6 fxe6 36 fxg6!** and White had a winning attack. How should the 35th moves be evaluated?

The answer is that both moves deserve double question marks. What the players saw was 35...♗xe1 36 exf7+ ♔xf7 37 fxg6+. What they overlooked was 36...♕xf7! with an easy win.

But 35 e6?? was not justified. And the reason has nothing to do with 35...♗xe1.

It was unwarranted because White was not lost when he played it. With the routine 35 ♖e2! he would stop 35...♖d2 and make 36 e6! a real threat. Chances would be roughly even.

In other words, 35 e6 was a gamble. It was certainly not a case of "nothing to lose," nor was it the most practical move.

Of course, a move can be both computer-best and practical. We saw that with Marshall's 19 ♕xc7! at the start of this chapter. Here's another example.

de Firmian – Thingstad
Tromso 2007

Black to play

In this battle between a veteran grandmaster and a 14-year-old amateur, the GM threatened to queen the h-pawn.

He also has tactics directed at the black king. He would win after 45...♕f8 46 ♕a7+ or 46 ♕c7+ or even 46 ♕g1. His position is that good.

Black played **45...b4!**. It is the best try in a lost position and threatens 46...♕d1+ and 47...b3 mate.

A false trail is 46 ♕a7+ ♔b5 47 ♕b7+? ♔a4!. White's advantage has evaporated as the best continuation shows, 38 ♕xb4+! ♕xb4 39 axb4 ♖d1+ 40 ♔a2 ♖h1.

Play went **46 axb4+! ♔xb4**.

White to play

This gives White something to think about. Can he finally deliver mate with 47 ♕b7+ ?

No, but 47...♔c5 48 b4+ cxb3 49 ♖c3+ would win. So would 48 ♖h3 with the idea of 49 ♖h5+.

What about eliminating checks with 47 ♔a2 ? That is a very appealing safety move and it also wins.

But the swindle succeeded after **47 h8(♕)+??** because White counted on **47...♕d1+ 48 ♔a2 ♕a4+ 49 ♖a3**.

He didn't see **48...♕b3+!** which mates (49 ♖xb3 cxb3+ 50 ♔d1 ♖d1).

Anti-Principle

The would-be swindler also has to overcome a fear of violating the basic principles of chess. Tactics trump principles in any swindle attempt.

Lilienthal – Tolush
Pärnu 1947

Black to play

Computers urge 23...♖f8?. But only **23...♖e1~** offered hope.

It violates a basic principle that says a player who has lost the Exchange should try to retain rooks. But the only tactical weakness White has is his first rank and the f2 square, and they are protected by his f1-rook.

Black threatens 24...♖xf1+ 25 ♔xf1 ♗h3+ and mates. He allowed 24 ♗xf7+ but after 24...♔h8 there is no immediate followup.

Better to delay a capture on f7 with **24 h4!**.

A principle worth following in Swindle-Think is to avoid a trade of queens. That's why Black rejected the computer-endorsed 24...♕e2, which runs out of gas after 25 ♕xe2 ♖xe2 26 ♖xf7 and ♔g2.

The swindler's move is **24...♕c1~**.

White to play

Computers are right in saying 25 ♕g2! leaves Black only one follow-up, 25...♗d3.

They are also right that it should lose after 26 ♖xe1 ♕xe1+ 27 ♔h2 because of 27...♗xf2?? 28 ♖xf7!.

But many humans have a problem with retreats like 25 ♕g2. White's first mistake was **25 ♖xe1?** because on **25...♕xe1+** he cannot play the natural 26 ♔g2? in view of 26...♗xf2! 27 ♕xf2 ♗h3+ 28 ♔f3 ♗g4+ with perpetual check.

Nevertheless, **26 ♔h2 ♗xf2 27 ♕g2** kept a semblance of a white advantage.

The best tactical try was 27...♕e2!. It threatens 28...♗xg3+ 29 ♔xg3 ♕e5!+ with perpetual check.

Instead, Black played a, move-to-confuse, **27...♔g7**.

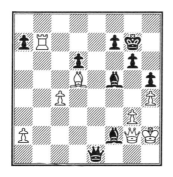

White to play

It prompts White to consider two ways of capturing on f7. Black was hinting that his king will be safe after 28 ♖xf7+ ♔h6. And he's right. White would have to make slow progress then.

It seemed to make more sense to play **28 ♗xf7** and threaten to trade bishops with 29 ♗e6+ and 30 ♗xf5.

There also seemed to be a mate after the natural 28...♔h6 is met by 29 ♗g8. (That's wrong: 29...♗xg3+! 30 ♕xg3 ♕d2+ leads to perpetual check. Or 29...♗g1+ as in the game.)

But 28 ♗xf7? was White's second error because **28...♗g1+! 29 ♕xg1 ♕e2+** is either another perpetual check or a drawish endgame.

A draw was reached soon after **30 ♕g2 ♕xg2+ 31 ♔xg2 ♗e4+ 32 ♔f2 ♗xb7 33 ♗e8 ♗a6 34 ♔e3 ♗xc4 35 a3 ♗f7 36 ♗b5 ♔f6 37 ♔d4 g5**.

Lost, Loster, Lostest

Before the computer era, it was often difficult to distinguish different degrees of disadvantage. We couldn't be sure whether a move made a lost position "loster."

Now we can tell the difference mathematically. But to a would-be swindler this is a distinction without a real difference. If a position is truly lost, a swindle try is worth it. This was something Frank Marshall understood.

Marshall – Tchigorin
Ostende 1907

White to play

Black threatens a quick mate with 23...bxc3 (24 bxc3? ♕a3 mate). He is only slightly slowed by 23 cxb4 ♕xb4, threatening ...♕xb2 mate.

Computers agree that White is dead lost. They only differ in evaluating the size of his disadvantage, from -4.00 to -7.00.

They recommend minimizing moves that are ludicrous to human eyes.

Stockfish suggests 23 ♘b1 and then 23...b3! 24 ♗h7+. By convincing Black to close the queenside, White might last an extra dozen or so moves.

Marshall played the only move that offered hope, **23 ♘xc4~**.

He was not counting on the crude blunder 23...♗xc4?? 24 ♕xa5. No, he wanted to see where the attacked queen would go.

It didn't seem to matter. Black would win quickly after 23...♕a1+ 24 ♗b1? bxc3 and the game would go on for a while after 24 ♔d2 ♕a2.

More accurate would be the immediate 23...♕a2. The knight on c4 is attacked and the end could come after 24 ♘e3 bxc3 25 bxc3 ♘e4 threatening ...♕b2 mate. Or after 24 ♘d2 bxc3 or 24 ♘d6 bxc3 25 bxc3 ♖b2.

In other words, 23...♕a1+ (or 23...♕a2) make a lost position "loster." Marshall could safely resign then. But he wanted to see if White would play it.

Black, one of the world's best players, replied with the good but less forcing **23...♕a6**. The difference gave Marshall a chance for **24 ♖xh6~**.

Black to play

This was a move-to-confuse. Black would still win after 24...gxh6 25 ♕xf6 but his task would be a bit harder. For example, 25...bxc3 and then 26 ♕xh6 ♕a1+ 27 ♗b1 ♗e4! (27 ♕g5+ ♗g6).

Instead, Black chose a good alternative – in fact, the computer-best move, **24...bxc3!**. Engines say his advantage has grown to about -9.00.

It grew to double digits after **25 ♖dh1~**. We are going beyond "loster." After 25...♕a1+ 26 ♗b1 gxh6 the evaluation is getting to "ridiculously lost."

But Black decided to increase it just a bit more with **25...gxh6**. The only consistent White move was **26 ♖xh6~**.

Black to play

Some computers give an evaluation of more than -30.00 (!) after 26...♕a1+ 27 ♗b1 cxb2+. For instance, 28 ♔c2 ♗e4+.or 28 ♔d2 ♘e4+ 29 ♔e3 ♖b3+.

But for several moves Black had been looking at variations in which he got to capture on b2. Here he jumped at **26...cxb2+??** and then realized that he was lost after **27 ♔d2!** (27...♖fc8 28 ♕xf6).

The game ended with **27...♘e4+ 28 ♗xe4 ♗xe4 29 ♕h8 mate**.

Third Best

But, you may be thinking, that was played when even grandmasters were horrible defenders. Today a world-class would never get away with intentionally playing third-best moves.

We will examine the swindling skill of a modern world champion in Chapter 11. But we'll end this chapter with another dramatic game and see how good you are at identifying best moves.

Play over the first 25 moves carefully without a computer. Try to figure out how many of White's moves and Black's moves from 14 ...♘xc4 to 25...h5 were "computer-best."

Portisch – Tal
Amsterdam 1964

1 ♘f3 ♘f6 2 g3 d6 3 d4 g6 4.♗g2 ♗g7 5 0-0 0-0 6 c4 ♗g4 7 ♘c3 ♕c8 8 ♖e1 ♖e8 9 ♕b3 ♘c6 10 d5 ♘a5 11 ♕a4 b6 12 ♘d2 ♗d7 13 ♕c2 c6 14 b4 ♘xc4 15 ♘xc4 cxd5 16 ♘a3 d4 17 ♗xa8 ♕xa8 18 ♘cb5 ♖c8 19 ♕d1 ♘e4 20 f3 a6 21 ♘xd4 ♕d5 22 ♗e3 ♖c3 23 ♘dc2 ♕f5 24 g4 ♕e6 25 ♗d4 h5

Take your time, an hour or more. After all, it took the players, two of the world's very best, about four hours to play them.

This was an important game for both players. It took place in the tournament that allowed White for the first time to advance to the Candidates stage of the world championship. It also permitted Black to come close to regaining his championship title.

Time's up. The answer is that most computers regard White's play as stellar. They say he made the correct decision at every crucial point, including when he made the moves 14 b4!, 16 ♘a3!, 18 ♘cb5!, 19 ♕d1!, 21 ♘xd4!, 22 ♗e3!, 23 ♘dc2! and 25 ♗d4!.

But the same engines considered most of the key moves by Black to be second- or third-best. Yet he drew the game.

Black to play

First, he chose **14...♘xc4~**, a sacrifice of a knight for two pawns. This turned a slightly inferior and passive position into a distinctively bad one. But it had the practical benefit of granting Black the initiative for the foreseeable future.

He increased the ante with **16...d4~**, which engines say is clearly worse than 16...♗f5 or 16...a5.

They acknowledge that Black would also be in major trouble after those "best" moves. For example, 16...♗f5 17 ♕d2 ♘e4 18 ♘xe4 ♗xa1 19 ♕xd5 is a big White edge, despite the nearly equal material.

Black's **19...♘e4~** is rated second or third best, after 19...a5 and 19...♘g4, by various machines – which concede Black would still be in bad shape.

It is worth noting that the first White move that comes under serious cyber-criticism is 20 f3. Some engines prefer 20 ♘xd4.

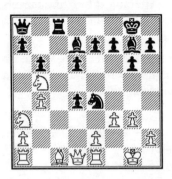

Black to play

Computers tend to rate **20...a6~** third best.

Some say 20...♘c3 21 ♘xc3 dxc3 was best and they conclude White is winning after 22 ♘c2 or 22 ♗g5.

Others prefer 20...d3 21 ♖b1 ♖xc1 22 ♖xc1 d2 – but recognize that 23 fxe4 dxe1(♕)+ 24 ♕xe1 is another winning edge for White.

They are back in unison about **21...♕d5~**, which they say is inferior to 21...♘c3. (Yet they admit Black would be losing after 21...♘c3 22 ♕d2 ♕d5 23 ♘dc2 or 23 e3.)

Engines can't see a good reason for **22...♖c3~**. They want Black to try 20...♗h3 or 20...♘c3.

Humans would understand that Black should not exchange queens when he is down so much material. But engines dislike **23...♕f5~** and recommend 23...♘f6. And two moves later:

Black to play

Some computers say the best Black can get is 25...♖xa3 26 ♘xa3 ♘c3 – but admit that then Black loses after 27 ♗xc3 ♗xc3 28 ♕d3.

Others say 25...♘g5 is the best try. After 26 ♕d2 they recommend 26...♘e4 but concede that almost any reasonable White move would end the struggle shortly.

Tal played **25...h5~** and after **26 &xg7** he did not recapture but went for **26...hxg4~**. How did he get away with this? White's advantage has grown to more than +8.00.

The answer is complex. First, his moves had cost White an enormous amount of time. Almost every Tal response was a surprise that required him to burn minutes to reconsider the position.

But it wasn't just that. Black had raised the luck level by creating unfamiliar tactical situations. White could easily play logical moves such as 27 &xc3 g3 28 hxg3 and discover that 28...Wh3! secures at least perpetual check.

White was beginning to miss knockout moves, such as 28 Wd4! ©xc3 29 hxg3! instead of 28 hxg3?? in that variation.

It was impossible to tell at the time but **27 ©d4? Wd5 28 fxe4 Wxe4** improved Black's chances considerably. But a rook and two pieces down, he was still lost.

White to play

White worried about perpetual check (29...We3+ 30 &h1 &c6+! 31 ©xc6 We4+ and draws). But rather than finish off with 29 e3! or 29 &h6 he tried to give back material.

Tal wouldn't take it. After **29 ©f3 We3+ 30 &h1** he rejected 30...gxf3 31 exf3 Wxf3+ or 30...&xg7 31 ©c2 Wf4 32 Wd4+ because a trade of queens would mean a lost endgame.

Instead, **30...&c6~** prompted White's most serious error.

He saw that 31 &xc3?? gxf3 would lose so he protected f3 further, **31 &f1**.

In crazy positions, a defender, even an elite grandmaster, leans towards such safety moves rather than trying to calculate complex continuations such as 31 Wd4 or 31 ©c2. (They would have won quickly.)

But remember Tartakower. Black did not punish 31 &f1?? with 31...gxf3 32 exf3 &xg7. Then he would have had the better chances after 33 ©c2 &xf3+ 34 &xf3 Wxf3+ 35 Wxf3 &xf3.

Instead, he played **31...♖xa3??**, the next-to-last error. The game's outcome might have turned around one more time after **32 ♖c1!**.

But White went for a draw and the game ended with **32 ♕c1 gxf3 33 ♕xc6 ♕xe2! 34 ♖g1 ♔xg7 35 ♖ae1 ♕d2 36 ♖d1 ♕e2 37 ♖de1 ♕d2 38 ♖d1 ♕e2 39 ♖de1 draw**.

The draw was called another example of Mikhail Tal's outrageous luck. In retrospect it was highly flawed case of precise, computer-best moves being contested by practical moves – in a game played by humans, not computers.

Quiz

Now let's see if you can think like a swindler.

4.

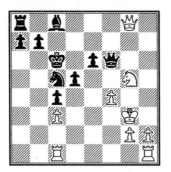

Burn – Marshall
Ostend 1906

White to play

White could win by pushing his h-pawn put preferred **31 ♕c8+** so that 31...♔c7 32 **♕f7+!** trades queens and wins the endgame.

How did Marshall respond to that?

5.

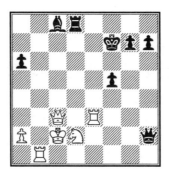

Smith – Laznicka
King of Prussia 2010

Black to play

Computers recommend moves like 38...h5 and 38...h6. What is more hopeful?

6.

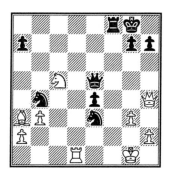

Bradford – Byrne
Greeneville 1980

White to play

Black was waiting for 30 ♗xb4 ♘xd1 31 ♕xe4 ♘e3! and mates.

White had a choice between 30 ♕xe4 and 30 ♘d7. Which is the swindler's choice?

Chapter Three:
Traps

Swindlers set traps. Some traps are crude. They are denigrated as "cheap" and "coffeehouse." But even celebrated players have been guilty of trying the crudest when they have nothing to lose.

Nimzovich – Kashdan
Bled 1931

White to play

White spent most of the last ten moves giving checks to prevent the advance of Black's pawns. The checks run out after 53 ♕e3+ ♔b7.

Before resigning Aron Nimzovich played **53 ♕d4+**. It's the kind of move you might expect from a beginner.

But Black had spent the last several moves looking for safe squares for his king. He might have moved quickly and overlooked **53...♕xd4!**.

He didn't. He played it and White **resigned**.

Some players would consider 53 ♕d4+ unbecoming of a master. But when the alternative is resigning, nothing is unbecoming in Swindle-think. There was simply no better move.

Here is a more difficult case.

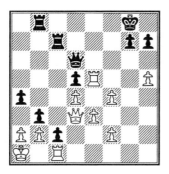

Gleizerov – Krasenkow
Groningen 2016

Black to play

Black can win with 34...a3 and ...axb2+. The short variation is 35 bxa3 b2 mate.

A longer one runs 35 axb3 axb2+ 36 ♔xb2 ♖a8!, threatening ...♕a3 mate.

But the fastest way to win was also the prettiest, **34...♕a3!**. It threatens ...♕xa2 mate and would again mate after 35 bxa3 b2.

Before resigning White can give checks. There is little point to 35 ♕xh7+ because there is virtually no chance that Black would fail to play 35...♔xh7!. This is not a trap.

But **35 ♖e8+!** was. It was possible Black would become confused and allow 35...♖xe8?? 36 bxa3.

Or a perpetual check might appear after **35...♔f7!**. But White resigned when he saw that 36 ♕f5+ ♔xe8 37 ♕e5+ ♕e7 ends the checks. Or 37 ♕e6+ ♔f8 38 ♕f5+ ♔g8.

Percentage Plays

Before resigning it often pays to give your opponent one last decision to make. Here's an extreme example.

van der Wiel – Short
Wijk an Zee 1990

Black to play

White has just played ♗g3-f4, with a decisive threat of ♖xh6 mate. Black tried **45...♕g3+.**

You might call this an "80-percent trap." There are five legal replies. Four of them, that is, 80 percent, would help Black.

On 46 ♔xg3 or 46 fxg3 Black is stalemated.

If White is so shocked by 45...♕g3+, he might even move his king and allow 46 ...♕xf4!.

Unfortunately, all it takes is one good answer to refute 45...♕g3+. Black resigned after **46 ♗xg3!.**

Black was a world-class player and knew the chances of success after 45...♕g3+ were not really one out of five. It was more of a joke move. But in more sophisticated examples, it pays to try a desperation move. Here is...well, a 75-percent trap.

Topalov – Kramnik
Las Vegas 1999

Black to play

White has just pushed his powerful extra pawn to d6. Black can try to defend with 37...♖d8 and 38 d7 ♕e6 39 ♕c7 ♖bb8. That would make his pieces somewhat passive.

Computers tend to say that policy is best. They would be right – if White had plenty of time. But both players had seconds left to reach the next time control, four moves away. Black tried **37...♖8b5.**

This looked excellent because White's queen is overworked. Throwing in a check, 38 ♕c8+ ♔h7, doesn't help because 39...♖f5+ and 39...♖h5 are still threatened.

White would be thrown on the defensive after 38 ♕c4 ♖f5+ 39 ♔g1 ♕e3+ 40 ♔h1 ♖f2. He would have to find a way to stop 41...♖xh2+! 42 ♔xh2 ♕xg3+.

Nevertheless, there was a powerful defense, **38 ♖c4!.**

Black to play

Now we can see that 37...♖8b5?? was a blunder. Black no longer has a piece to safely guard his first rank.

He would lose quickly after 38...♕g6 39 ♕c8+ ♔h7 40 d7. Computers consider that his best chance because it minimizes his material deficit: He would only be a rook down after 40...♖b8 41 d8(♕) ♖xc8 42 ♕xc8.

Humans don't play minimizing moves. Black replied **38...♖f3+~**.

There are four legal moves. We can quickly dispose of 39 ♔g2?? because 39...♕xe2 is check and will be followed by a winning 40...♖xc5.

White to play

A little harder to work out is 39 exf3. It becomes easier when you see that the only real forcing moves are 39...♖b2+! 40 ♔g1 ♕xf3.

Then Black threatens mate with ...♕g2 or ...♕xd1. White would be much worse after 41 ♕c8+ ♔h7 42 ♕h3 ♕xd1+ 43 ♕f1 ♕d5.

The third possibility was **39 ♔g1?? ♕xe2**. White can resign – and he did after **40 ♕d4 ♖b2**. (Or 40 ♕c8+ ♔h7 41 ♖dc1 ♖b2 42 ♖4c2 ♕e3+! 43 ♔g2 ♕xc1 and 43 ♔h1 ♖f2.)

But the fourth move would have won, 39 ♔e1!.

Then Black's queen and a rook are hanging. The d-pawn would finally score after 39...♖c3 40 ♖xe4 ♖3xc5 41 d7.

Even more desperate is 39...♖f1+ so that 40 ♔xf1? ♕h1+ prolongs the game. But much simpler is 40 ♖xf1 ♖xc5 41 ♖xe4.

This doesn't excuse a blunder (37...♖8b5??). But it once again shows that desperate times call for desperate measures – and only the last blunder matters.

Best-Move Traps

Some traps aren't even "trappy." They arise out of solid moves in good positions.

For example, after **1 d4 d5 2 c4 e6 3 ♘c3 ♘f6 4 ♗g5** Black has ample choice of fine moves, including 4...♗e7 and 4...c6. They seem appropriate because White's last move appeared to threaten to win a pawn.

However, **4...♘bd7** is quite a good alternative. Then on **5 cxd5 exd5**:

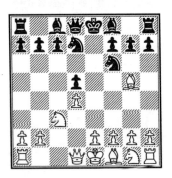

White to play

Now **6 ♘xd5?** is a blunder because the pin does not hold: **6...♘xd5!** and 7 ♗xd8 ♗b4+! regains the queen at the profit of an extra piece (8 ♕d2 ♗xd2+ 9 ♔xd2 ♔xd8).

Compare that with **1 e4 e5 2 ♘f3 ♘c6 3 ♗c4 ♘d4?**.

White to play

This sets a trap that beginners often fall into.

They see that 4 ♘xe5 would win a pawn and threaten a capture on f7. But **4 ♘xe5 ♛g5! 5 ♘xf7? loses to 5...♛xg2 6 ♖f1 ♛xe4+ 7 ♗e2 ♘f3 mate**.

There is a fundamental difference between 3...♘d4? and the previous example's 4...♘bd7. This one is a bad move. White can get a clear advantage with, for example, 4 c3 or 4 ♘xd4 exd4 5 0-0. In contrast, there is nothing at all wrong with 4...♘bd7 in the previous example.

Good players – and this includes good swindlers – rarely play opening moves that they *know* are bad or even second best. Those kinds of traps may win an occasional game among less experienced opponents. But if you improve as a player, you will face better opponents and they will punish your crude traps.

Endgame Traps

In many basic endgames there are coffeehouse traps. But there are also good moves which also set traps. Often they are the best moves.

White to play

Masters would say this is a "dead draw" because the best moves make it so. But masters know that **1 ♔d6!** is a valid winning try.

It makes a threat (2 ♖a8+ ♔f7 3 e6+ and then 3...♔f6 4 ♖f8+ ♔g7 5 e7 wins).

But 1 ♔d6 also sets two traps. One is 1...♖h6+?? and 2 e6. Then White threatens ♖a8 mate and he can clear a path for his pawn (2...♔f8 3 ♖a8+ ♔g7 4 ♔d7 and 5 e7 wins).

The second trap is 1...♖d1+?? 2 ♔e6! (2...♔f8 3 ♖a8+ ♔g7 4 ♔e7 and 5 e6 is a win).

To draw after 1 ♔d6, Black has to know the book theory or work out it out at the board. There is only one drawing move, **1...♖e1!**. Black can meet 2 ♖a8+ ♔f7 3 e6+ with 3...♖xe6+.

White to play

White has one way to try to win, **2 ♔e6!**. It threatens 3 ♖a8 mate.

Black can draw with a king move. For example, **2...♔f8 3 ♖a8+ ♔g7**.

White has one last bid to win, **4 ♔d6!**. He threatens 5 e6!.

There is only one defense, **4...♔f7!** draws. (White would eventually win after 4...♖d1+?? 5 ♔e7! and 6 e6!.)

But no master would say that 1 ♔d6!, 2 ♔e6! and 4 ♔d6! set deep traps. They were simply the best available moves.

Endgame Swindles

Endgame swindles occur when a defender is genuinely lost and has no resource except to set traps. Masters know they should try them, even against a future world champion.

Carlsen – Radjabov
Bazna 2010

Black to play

White threatens to queen after moving his rook, to a8, b8, d8 – or even to e8 and f8.

The only drawing chance seems to be 63...♔d7 because by attacking the rook, Black wins the c-pawn.

But Black knew a basic winning technique in similar endings. After 63...♔d7 White can play 64 ♖d8+! ♔xc7 and then 65 ♖d2 cuts Black's king off from the kingside.

Black to play

White has a simple winning plan of pushing his f-pawn. For example, 65...♔c6 66 f5 ♔c7 67 f6 ♔c6 68 ♖f2! and f6-f7.

Using his rook, 66...♖f1 67 ♔g5 ♖g1+, doesn't help Black. White would win with 68 ♔f6 followed by ♔f7, f5-f6 and so on.

In other words, Black is lost whatever he does in the previous diagram. Computers tell us the best way to prolong the game is 63...♖h1+ 64 ♔g5 ♖g1+. After 65 ♔f5 Black has no more checks. White is still ready to queen after a rook move. Black can resign.

But a swindler always hesitates before he resigns. Is there a trap I can set? Black found one, **63...♖c1!**.

White to play

He was hoping that White would remember an endgame tactic that wins in similar positions:

After 64 ♖g8 it appears that the only way to prevent queening is 64...♖xc7.

But that allows White to trade rooks, 65 ♖g7+ ♔d8 66 ♖xc7 ♔xc7. Then his king shepherds his f-pawn to the eighth rank, 67 ♔g5 ♔d7 68 ♔f6 ♔e8 69 ♔g7 and 70 f5, 71 f6 and so on.

But 64 ♖g8?? would fall into the trap. Black would turn the tables with 64...♖h1+! 65 ♔-moves ♖g1+ and 66...♖xg8 wins. (This is why 64 ♖h8?? ♖h1+ is also a blunder.)

White avoided the trap with **64 ♔g5**. There were no more traps to set, so Black **resigned**. The rest could have been 64...♖g1+ 65 ♔f5 ♖c1 and now that tactic works, 66 ♖h8! (or 66 ♖g8!) ♖xc7 67 ♖h7+.

Traps are tools. Players set them when they are trying to get the advantage in an even position and when they are trying to win an advantageous position faster. But in this book we are interested in the traps you can set when you are trying to save a bad or lost position. They are the tools that can make you lucky.

Quiz

Setting a trap is often a risky business as these positions show.

7.

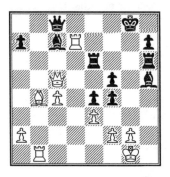

Tal – Saigin
Riga 1954

Black to play

In a seesaw game, White regained the initiative.

Some computers recommend 42...♖e5 with drawing chances in the endgame after 43 ♕xc7 ♕xc7 44 ♖xc7 fxe3.

But then they see a better move for Black. Which?

8.

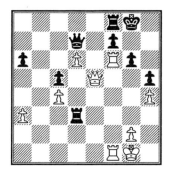

Andersson – Velimirovic
Szirak 1987

Black to play

Black can get adequate counterplay with 28...♖e8, to stop ♕e7. For example, 29 ♕xc5 ♖e2 and 30...♖dd2 with ...♖xg2+ in mind.

He chose the immediate **28...♖d2**. What trap does that set? Is it a good move?

Bobby Fischer set a faulty trap in this game.

9.

Fischer – Udovcic
Bled 1961

White to play

Fischer played **37 b5.**

(a) What is the trap?

(b) Is it sound?

(c) Was there a better move?

10.

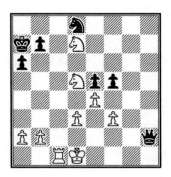

Short – Palac
Gibraltar 2003

White to play

White was lost for most of the middlegame. Now he has a choice between 33 ♘e7 and 33 ♖c8. What traps would they set?

Chapter Four:
Make Yourself Lucky

There are three basic ways to maximize your chances of a successful swindle:

(a) Identify your best tactical resources,

(b) Give your opponent choices, and

(c) Confuse him.

It should be no surprise that a swindle is fueled by tactics. While an opponent is trying to convert a winning material or positional advantage, the would-be swindler is looking for ways to conjure up surprise checks, captures and threats.

José Capablanca is not remembered as a swindler. But he carried off some great ones, such as this.

Fine – Capablanca
AVRO 1938

Black to play

White is a pawn up and about to win at least another one, thanks to fxe5.

But Black has hidden counterchances based on the potential vulnerability of g2.

A natural defense is 24...♖d8, protecting the d4-pawn in case of 25 fxe5 ♕xe5. That would also set a subtle trap:

White may be tempted to win a pawn with 26 ♕h6+ ♖g7 27 ♖xf6+?.

But after 27...♔g8 he lacks a good way of meeting the threat of ...♖xg2+.

White to play

For example, 28 g3 ♗b7! and ...♕d5 favors Black.

And 28 ♖f2 ♗xg2! leads to 29 ♖xg2 ♖xg2+ 30 ♔xg2 ♖d6.

Then 31 ♕h4? ♖g6+ 32 ♔f1 ♖f6+ wins and 31♕h3! ♖g6+ 32 ♔f1 ♖f6+ draws by perpetual check.

But this is much too optimistic. White can answer 24...♖d8 with 25 ♖e1!.

Then he is threatening 26 fxe5 ♕xe5 27 ♕h6+ (27...♖g7 28 ♖xe4!). Black's position would be hopeless because he has no obvious counterplay.

But he has a better way of making a capture on g2 credible. To make that work better he needed reinforcements and began with **24...♔f7!**.

White to play

This looks like a routine defensive move, protecting the f-pawn and avoiding ♕h6 with check.

But it was a warning alarm to White. When he began to consider 25 fxe5 he saw that Black had prepared 25...♖xg2+! 26 ♖xg2 ♗xg2.

Then 27 ♔xg2?? ♖g8+ allows mate and 27 ♕xg2 ♖g8 costs the queen.

White could try for an edge with 27 ♕f2 or 27 ♘xd4 instead. But he deserves a clearer advantage than that, considering his position one move ago.

He chose **25 ♖e1!**. It threatens to win with 26 fxe5 ♕xe5 27 ♖f4 (27...f5 28 ♖exe4!). He has a second threat, 26 ♘c5 (26...♗c6 27 fxe5!).

Black's situation is so dire that some computers recommend 25...♖xg2+? 26 ♖xg2 ♗xg2. But they concede he would have scant compensation after 27 ♔xg2 ♖g8+ 28 ♔h1.

If he felt his position was hopeless, Black might go into that variation anyway and set a desperation trap with 28...♖g4.

At first it looks just like Black intends 29...♖xf4 and 30...♖f1+.

But the trap would be sprung by 29 fxe5?? ♕f3+ or 29 ♖f1?? ♕e4+, with mate to follow.

Capablanca rejected 28...♖g4 because it would be too easy to find a favorable defense. After 29 ♕d3 or 29 ♕e2 he would have slim compensation for his lost piece. He wasn't *that* desperate.

Black to play

He was lost but not done thinking about g2. He found **25...♖g4~**, so that his other rook can get into play at g8.

This also enables him to meet 26 fxe5! ♕xe5 27 ♕xd4? ♕xd4 28 ♘xd4 with 28...♗xg2!.

Then 29 ♖xg2 ♖xd4 would reach a pawn-down endgame that he might be able to hold.

But White can improve on 27 ♕xd4 in two ways, one of them complex, the other easier to calculate.

White to play

The first defense is 27 ♘xd4! so that 27...♖ag8 28 ♘f3! blocks the bishop.

That doesn't end his tactical weakness at g2. Black can try 28...♕f5 29 ♕e3 ♗xf3 and only 30 ♖xf3 wins.

Much easier to calculate is 27 h3!. This also wins because the rook is kicked off its ideal square.

Black would lose after 27...♖g3 or 27...♖h4 because now 28 ♕xd4! is safe. And 28 ♘xd4! is even better after 27...♖h4.

But as he examined 26 fxe5 White also wondered about the other threat he had when he played 25 ♖e1. He chose **26 ♘c5**.

If the attacked bishop retreats (26...♗c6) then 27 fxe5 is crushing because the Black queen is attacked.

Black to play

What White missed was **26...♗xg2! 27 ♖xg2 ♖ag8!**.

The turnaround would be complete after 28 ♖xg4?? ♕xg4+ 29 ♔f1 ♕h3+ and Black wins.

When White recovered from the shock he found **28 ♖e2**. It keeps his extra piece and might have won after 28...♖xf4 29 ♕d1.

But Black had compensation after **28...exf4**. He threatened 29...♕xc5 as well as 29...f3.

Suddenly it looked like Black was winning (29 ♕a5 f3 30 ♕xa7+ ♔g6).

But **29 ♘b7!** threatened a fork at d6 and kept the balance, **29...♕d5 30 ♖xg4 ♖xg4+ 31 ♗g2 ♖xg2+ 32 ♕xg2 f3** and now 33 ♘d6+! ♕xd6 34 ♕xf3.

The game actually went **33 ♕h3? ♕g5+ 34 ♕g3 ♕c1+ 35 ♔f2 ♕e3+** and *White* was lucky to draw.

Black survived because he identified his chief tactical target, g2, and took the preparatory measures (...♔f7, ...♖g4) necessary to exploit it. White helped him by forgetting about the vulnerability of g2 (with 26 ♘c5??).

Psychology of a Swindle

A surprise attack along the g-file is also a theme of the following game. It illustrates how the psychology of a swindle begins. In the first diagram, White was thinking "How do I finish him off?" Within a few moves he needed to switch to "Whoops! I'm no longer winning easily. I have to be more careful." But he couldn't mentally reset.

Ivanchuk – Topalov
Las Palmas 1996

1 e4 c5 2 ♘f3 d6 3 d4 cxd4 4 ♘xd4 ♘f6 5 ♘c3 a6 6 ♗e3 e6 7 g4 h6 8 f4 b5 9 ♗g2 ♗b7 10 g5 hxg5 11 fxg5 b4 12 ♘a4 ♘h5 13 0-0 ♘d7? 14 g6! ♘hf6 15 c3! ♘e5 16 gxf7+ ♔xf7 17 cxb4

Black to play

Black is a pawn down and his king is vulnerable because of potential threats to capture the e6-pawn.

For example, 17...♖c8 18 ♕b3 and now 18...♕d7? 19 ♘b6 loses. On 18...♕e7 White can play 19 ♗g5 followed by 20 h4 and ♗h3!.

It makes sense to block the b3-e6 diagonal with 18...♘c4. But that allows 19 ♘xe6! ♔xe6 20 ♘c5+ with a winning attack (20...bxc5 21 ♕xc4+ ♔e7 22 ♖ad1 or 22 e5).

Computers propose grim defensive measures for Black such as 17...♕e7 18 ♕b3 ♖e8 or 17...♖b8 18 ♕b3 ♗c8.

Black looked beyond defense. He saw that there were things he could attack after **17...♖h4~**.

White to play

He was trying to make ...♗xe4 possible – and to make it stronger after ...♖g4.

But this should not succeed. With 18 ♗f4 and ♗g3 White would block the g-file.

His advantage would be as great after 18 ♗f4 ♖g4 19 ♗g3 (19...♗xe4? 20 ♗h3!) as if Black had played a computer-endorsed move like 17...♕e7.

But like White in the previous example, he felt there should be something more immediate.

He looked at *his* best tactical resource, a possible capture on e6 that would lead to a quick knockout. The game went **18 ♕b3 ♕e8**.

White to play

Again 19 ♗f4! is safe, with the same idea as before, ♗g3 and ♗h3.

But Black's last move, 18...♕e8, suggested a new tactic to White. He might be able to check with a rook on c7 and win the b7-bishop.

After 19 ♖ac1 he could calculate 19...♖c8 20 ♖xc8 ♗xc8. Then 21 ♖c1 creates a new threat of ♖c7+.

This blinded him to **19 ♖ac1? ♗xe4!**. He needed to mentally reset himself.

If he had he would have chosen 20 ♖f4!. That is not a difficult move to find. Rather it is difficult to admit that after exchanges, 20...♖xf4 21 ♗xf4 ♗xg2 22 ♔xg2, he would no longer be winning.

In fact, with 22...♘d5! Black would guard the checking square, c7, and threaten ...♘xf4+. He would be at least equal.

But White continued to play as if he held all the high cards, with **20 ♖c7+?** **♔g8**.

White to play

Now 21 ♗xe4 ♖xe4 22 ♘xe6 would lose material to 22...♖xe3! 23 ♕xe3 ♕xe6.

So White played, **21 ♘xe6**, the capture he had been thinking about since moves 15-16.

There were tactical reasons to believe this might work, such as 21...d5 22 ♗xe4 ♖xe4 23 ♘ac5 or 21...♔h8 22 ♗xe4 ♖xe4 23 ♘f4.

Those variations don't favor White significantly. But what he overlooked is that Black got to carry out the idea *he* had been thinking about since move 17:

White was lost after **21...♖g4!**.

61

White to play

Too late, White saw that 22 ♘g5+?? loses outright to 22...♗d5 because 23 ♗xd5+ is illegal.

Also lost is 22 ♘f4+ d5, when Black threatens 23...♘f3+ 24 ♔h1 ♘h4!, as well as 23...♘d3! and 23...♗xg2 24 ♘xg2 ♖xb4!.

White was still in shock. He completed the collapse with **22 ♖xf6??** **♖xg2+ 23 ♔f1**. He was grasping at straws, such as 23...gxf6 24 ♘g7+.

But he was mated by **23...♕b5+!**.

Choice of Targets

In the heat of battle, the best tactical resource may not be evident because there may be more than one candidate.

Black's main strength in the next example is his control of the c-file. But he looked elsewhere. His swindle worked only due to the mutual mistakes that often occur in swindles.

Nunn – I. Gurevich
Hastings 1992-3

Black to play

What is the weakest point in White's armor? It looks like the e4-pawn. It can be attacked by both of Black's rooks and perhaps the bishop as well.

But the sneaky defense is 39...♖hc8!. It seems to prepare 40...♖c4. The real point is a trap: 40 gxf6? allows 40...♖c3!.

That reveals that the weakest target in White's camp is actually the h3-pawn. The black rooks would be active enough to draw after 41 fxg7 ♖xh3+ 42 ♔g2 ♖g3+ 43 ♔f2 ♖c2+ 44 ♔e1 ♖h2 or 44...h3.

More of a test is 41 ♕d1 ♖xh3+ 42 ♔g1. (But not 42 ♔g2?? ♖8c3! and Black wins.)

Unfortunately for Black, 39...♖hc8! would not save him. He would be lost, for example, after 40 ♖g1 ♖c3 41 ♔h2 ♖8c4 42 ♕b6. Or 41...♖d3 42 ♕f2! and ♕xh4 – but not 42 ♕b6? ♖8c3.

Instead, he went for **39...♖e8?**. That made **40 gxf6!** strong.

The attack on the e4-pawn is too late, 40...♖c4 41 ♕b6 followed by fxg7 (or 40...gxf6 41 ♖g1!).

Black had to reply **40...gxf6**.

White to play

White is much closer to a win than in the previous diagram. How does he finish off? He can try to trade rooks and invade with his king, say at g4. Another good plan is to use his rook to create a mating attack.

He can advance both plans with 41 ♖g1! and a check on g7.

For example, 41...♖c4 42 ♖g7+ ♔c8? 43 ♕a7 and mates. White's king can flee checks (43...♖c1+ 44 ♔g2 ♖c2+ 45 ♔f3 ♖c3+ 46 ♔f4!).

If Black goes on defense, 41...♖f8 42 ♖g7+ ♔c8, he can hardly move because 43...♖c4? again loses to 44 ♕a7. Or 41...♖e7 42 ♕xf6 and ♖g7.

White went for a third plan, preparing to advance the f-pawn, after **41 ♕xf6**. Black seemed to have nothing better than **41...♖xe4**.

White to play

Consistent was 42 ♕g7+! because if Black moved his king, 43 f6 would win.

But it wasn't immediately obvious how to beat 42...♖e7. For example, 43 ♕g6 could prompt Black to discover the weakness at h3, with 43...♖c3!.

Then White isn't winning – 44 f6 ♖ee3! – and would be losing after 45 f7?? ♖xh3+.

Also bad is 43 ♕h8 in view of 43...♖xd5! 44 ♕xh4? ♗c6! followed by a discovered check.

There is a forcing win but it is hard to find, 43 ♕g4! ♗e2 44 ♕a4+! ♗b5 45 ♕xh4.

Instead, the game went **42 ♖g1 ♖xd5**.

White to play

This is a very difficult position to evaluate even when you have plenty of time. Black has a new tactical resource based on the c6-h1 diagonal.

But 43...♗c6 is not an immediate threat because Black needs c6 for his king. He would be losing after 44 ♖g7+ ♔c8 45 ♖g8+.

What should White do? He can try to mate with 43 ♖g7+ ♔c6 44 ♕d8 or 44 ♕f7. Analysis shows that either might have won.

White would probably also win after a safety-move such as 43 ♖g2.

But it seemed that 43 ♕f7+ would do the job faster after 43...♔c6 44 ♖c1+ (or 44 ♕g8).

What he overlooked was **43 ♕f7+?? ♖e7!**. The hot diagonal is fatally opened. If White moves his queen to g8, g6 or f8, Black sets up a crushing discovered check with 44...♗c6.

For example, 44 ♕g6 ♗c6 45 ♖f1 ♖d3+! 46 ♔g1 ♖g3+.

White played **44 ♕xd5 ♗c6 45 ♕g2** and **resigned** soon after **45...♗xg2+**.

Only after the game was it apparent that both players were so focused on the ...♖c4xe4 idea that they overlooked another. When White played 41 ♕xf6?? –

Black to play

Black played 41...♖xe4, but missed 41...♗d3!. Then White cannot stop 42...♗xe4+ and the outcome would be unclear.

Black didn't use his best tactical resources at first (39...♖hc8! and 41...♗d3!). But the position was so double-edged that he could afford to discover it later (...♗c6).

Give Your Opponent Choices

One of the common mistakes that a would-be swindler makes is relying on forcing moves.

This is a logical policy: If he keeps giving checks or threatening to capture enemy pieces, he limits his opponent's options. "Always check. It may be mate."

But in a genuinely bad position you are unlikely to have many *good* forcing moves. A better strategy is to get your opponent to make choices.

This sounds dumb. Why give your opponent a free hand? Well, you would be surprised what may happen, even if his choices seem simple.

65

Hanauer – Pavey
New York 1951

White to play

In this game from a US Championship, Black has a rook, two bishops and a pawn for his sacrificed queen. That's a huge edge, like having an extra piece.

Conservative defense (29 ♕c2, 29 ♕e1) may prolong the game. But it won't change the result unless Black blunders.

White increased the likelihood of a mistake with **29 ♕e7~**.

He was virtually daring his opponent to mate him. But he was giving Black a large menu of choices. For example, should he start with an obvious move, 29...♗d4+ ?

Then 30 ♔e1 ♗c3+ 31 ♔f2 ♖d2+ must be tightening the noose, right? But 30 ♔f3! isn't so clear.

Black reacted well, with **29...♖d2+!**. He saw that he may have a winning 30...♖e2+ if the king goes to e1 or e3.

White's best, sadly, was **30 ♔f3**.

Black to play

Black has a choice of forcing and non-forcing moves. The forcing moves are bishop checks at e2 and d5. For example, 30...♗d5+ 31 ♔e3? ♘c4 mate. But 31 ♔g4 requires further work.

The most appealing non-forcing moves are 30...h5 and 30...f5. They take away the White king's escape square at g4.

The game would be over after 30...f5! in view of 31...♗d5+ 32 ♔e3 ♘c4 mate. But the temptation to finish the game with forcing moves was great because they are the easiest to calculate. That explains **30...♗e2+**.

Then 31 ♔e4 ♖d4+ 32 ♔e3 ♘d5+ is *finis*. (Computers actually recommend 31 ♕xe2? ♖xe2 because it lengthens the game.)

The game went **31 ♔g2 ♗g4+!**. White could have resigned because each king move looked hopeless, 32 ♔e3 ♘d5+ or 32 ♔g1 ♗d4+.

But he had nothing to lose and chose **32 ♔f1**.

Black to play

Put yourself in Black's chair and you would be thinking, "There has to be a mate now."

You look at 32...♖d1+ and see that 33 ♔f2 ♗d4+ 34 ♔g2 ♖g1 is the mate you expected.

But 33 ♔g2 ♗d4 34 h3 is another spoiler.

You might also be disappointed when you look at 32...♗h3+ 33 ♔e1. (In fact, the non-forcing 33...♗c3! followed by a discovered check by the rook does the job.)

But **32...♗d4!** was at least as good. According to computers, White is going downhill. His position was lost, became "loster" and is on the verge of "lostest."

White to play

The threat is 33...♖d1+ 34 ♔g2 ♖g1 mate. Clearly 33 ♔e1 ♖d1 mate is no defense.

White played the only move to keep the game going, **33 h3**.

This sets a trap: If Black goes forcing with 33...♖d1+ 34 ♔g2 ♖g1+?? he discovers after 35 ♔h2 that he is worse.

White threatens 36 hxg4 and would meet 36...♗f3?? with 36 ♕d8+ and 37 ♕xd4+.

Aside from that blunder, Black had three attractive moves to choose from: 33...♗xh3+, 33...♗f3, and 33...♖f2+. Each seemed to end the game.

The rook check wins the queen after 34...♖e2+.

Also winning is 33...♗h3+ 34 ♔e1 ♗c3! because of the discovered check mentioned earlier.

Black may not have seen the key ...♗c3 move. Or he may have just concluded that **33...♗f3** was better because 34...♖d1+.

White to play

But the game ended **34 ♕e8+ ♔g7 35 ♘e6+! draw**.

There are perpetual queen checks at e7, e8, g5 and h4 after 35...fxe6.

This illustrates something we will explore in the next chapter. Players can get swindled when they focus on their own tactics and forget about their opponent's.

In the final position, Black can even lose after 35...♔f6?? 36 ♘xd4 ♖xd4 37 ♕e5 mate.

Or 35...♔h6?? 36 ♕f8+ ♔h5 and now 37 ♘xd4 ♖xd4? 38 ♕g7 (or 37 ♘g7+ ♗xg7 38 ♕xg7).

Black was victimized by having too many good moves. If he had had only one move that seemed to win – after 30 ♔f3, 32 ♔f1 or 33 h3 – he would probably have found it and played it quickly.

"After all," he might think, "why should I try to find a second win? You can only win a game once."

Defying the Odds

What is shocking about many swindles is that the victim had repeated opportunities to deal a fatal blow. The odds that he or she will miss one knockout punch seems high. The odds that it will happen again and again escalates sharply.

Yet practice shows that the swindler often defies the odds.

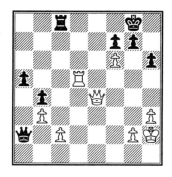

Paehtz – Tomilova
St. Petersburg 2009

Black to play

In mutual time pressure, Black blundered into this lost position. White threatens 38 ♕g4 and 39 ♕xg7 mate or 39 ♕xc8+. And 38...gxf6 39 ♕g4+ is no defense.

Some computers say 37...♕xc2 is best. So would some crude swindlers:

Then Black is betting that the opponent would fail to see 38 ♖d8+ ♖xd8 39 ♕xc2, with a winning endgame.

Good swindlers don't allow *simple* tactics like that.

Better is 37...♖b8 because White would have to work harder to find a knockout. It would take some calculation to see that 38 ♕f4 ♖a8 39 fxg7 – or 38 ♕g4 g6 39 ♕d4 – would win.

Black chose **37...g6**. Black threatens to equalize with 38...♕xc2 (39 ♖d8+ ♔h7!).

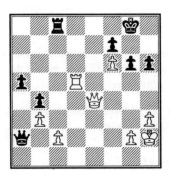

White to play

If White were told there were three forced wins, she might have found all three.

The methodical one is 38 ♕e7! and 39 ♖d8+. For example, 38...♕a1 39 ♖d8+ ♖xd8 40 ♕xd8+ ♔h7 41 ♕e7 ♔g8 42 ♕e8+ and mate, or 41...h5 42 h4.

Harder to see is 38 ♖d7! followed by ♖xf7!. It even works after 38...♖f8.

White found the computer-best win, beginning with **38 ♖c5!**. Then 38...♖xc5 39 ♕e8+ mates.

The attacked black rook doesn't have a good square. After 38...♖b8 White can play 39 ♕f4 and threaten ♕xb8+ but also ♕xh6 and mate on g7.

Black kept the game going at least a little longer with **38...♖f8**.

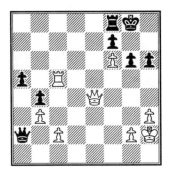

White to play

Thanks to her last move, White doesn't have to worry about ...♕xc2.

But that wouldn't matter anyway because 39 ♕e7! threatens 40 ♕xf8+! ♚xf8 41 ♖c8 mate. Black can resign after 39 ♕e7.

Instead, White played **39 ♖c7.** Why?

The best explanation is that it wins by force. It threatened 40 ♖xf7! ♖xf7 41 ♕e8+ or 40...♚xf7 41 ♕e7+ and mates.

Once she saw that, there didn't seem to be a reason to look for a second winning idea, 39 ♕e7!. "You can only win a game once," she might have said.

After 39 ♖c7, computers want Black to go into a hopeless ♕-vs-♖ endgame with 39...♕b2 40 ♖xf7 ♕xf6. But Black coolly played **39...g5!.**

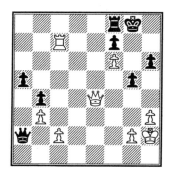

White to play

She is still lost. But she can avert mate after 40 ♖xf7 ♚xf7 41 ♕e7+ ♚g6!.

White would have to win a queen endgame after 42 ♕g7+ ♚h5 43 ♕xf8.

Even then there were chances for a trap. For example, 43...♕xc2 44 f7?? walks into 44...♕c7+!.

This leads to a stunning perpetual check, 45 g3 ♕c2+ or 45 ♚g1 ♕c1+ 46 ♚f2 ♕d2+ 47 ♚f3 ♕d3+.

But White's position is much better than a queen endgame. If the diagram carried a caption that read "White to play and mate," she would have found the tactic she missed on the previous move – 40 ♕e7! and ♕xf8+!.

White didn't look for a faster win because she found **40 h4.** Then 41 hxg5 hxg5 42 ♕f5 – or any queen move that threatens ♕xg5+ – looked decisive.

But Black was coming back from the dead after **40...♕a1!.**

71

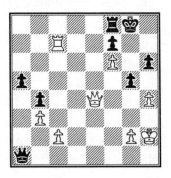

White to play

Now that the time control is reached, White could calculate more. Fortunately, she still has two wins. Unfortunately, the variations are much more complex:

Does 41 ♖xf7 win?

The answer is yes, 41...♔xf7 42 ♕e7+ ♔g7. But she would have to avoid 43 ♕xf8?? ♕e5+!, when Black has at least a perpetual check.

The win lies in 43 g4!, which threatens 44 ♕g7 mate or 44 h5 mate.

Does 41 ♕e7 win?

Again yes. But not after 41...♔h7! 42 ♕xf8?? ♕e5+!, with another perpetual check. It's a win after 42 ♖c4, 42 ♕e6 or 42 ♖c8, for example.

White took the easy way out, by heading into an apparently winning endgame, **41 hxg5? ♕d1! 42 ♖c5? ♕h5+ 43 ♔g3 hxg5 44 ♖xa5 ♕h4+ 45 ♕xh4 gxh4+ 46 ♔xh4.** But there were technical difficulties to solve as well as traps to avoid. She fell into one after **46...♖c8 47 ♖b5 ♖xc2 48 ♖xb4 ♔h7 49 ♖g4 ♖b2**

White to play

50 ♖g7+?? ♔h6 51 g4 ♖h2+ 52 ♔g3 ♖g2+! (53 ♔xg2 stalemate) and the game was soon drawn.

The final stalemate trick was an aftershock. But what was truly astonishing was the way White missed forced wins on moves 39, 40 and 41. And she had more than one way to force a win at each turn. But once she saw a strong move, she didn't look for a stronger one.

How Much is Enough?

Quite a different reason for giving your opponent choices is that he may not be certain what it takes to win a looming endgame. When he starts thinking about grabbing an extra pawn, he may self-destruct.

Lutz – Yusupov
Essen 2002

White to play

Would you consider 36 ♕xg2 or 36 ♖h2 if you were White? Of course not. It's crazy to trade queens when you are a piece down. Yet some computers say those moves are best.

When White looks for a tactical idea there is one that stands out. He chose **36 ♕h5~** because it threatens ♕f7 mate.

Black had something to think about because there was more than one way to parry it. The leading options were 36...♗e8 and 36...♕g6.

But when Black looks at 36...♗e8 he can see a nasty surprise, 37 ♕h6+!. Then 37...♘xh6 38 ♗e7 is a surprise mate.

Black can decline the sacrifice with 37...♘g7 but then 38 ♕h4 would threaten 39 ♗e7+ ♔f7 40 ♕f6 mate.

For example, 38...♕g6? loses to 39 ♗d8 ♕f7 and now 40 ♗xa5! and ♗b4+. Or 38...♕f3 39 ♗e7+ ♔f7 40 ♖h6!, threatening ♖f6+.

So after 38 ♕h4, would have to play 38...♗f7, allowing perpetual check, 39 ♗xg7+ ♖xg7 40 ♕d8+ ♗e8 41 ♖h8+ ♖g8 42 ♕f6+.

What this means is 36...♗e8? throws away an easy win and might even lose. Once he realizes that, Black can turn his attention turn to 36...♕g6.

73

But there is a third option, grabbing a pawn. Black doesn't really need an extra pawn to win. But he can do it with check. Play went **36...♕xf2+ 37 ♔c1.**

Black to play

Black still has to do something about ♕f7 mate. Again he has a choice.

One defense is 37...♕g1+ followed by 38...♕g6. This is better than 36...♕g6 would have been and not just in a material sense.

That f2-pawn played a defensive role for White. After 37...♕g1+ 38 ♔d2?? ♖g2+ he would be getting mated. And after 38 ♔b2 ♕g6 39 ♕h3 ♘e3! his king is the more vulnerable one (40 ♕xe3 ♕xh7 or 40 ♕h2 ♘d1+).

But once again Black saw something that looked better, **37...♕f4+ 38 ♔b2 ♗e8.**

White to play

Unlike the position when White played 36 ♕h5, now Black's queen is on f4, not g2. That means the 39 ♕h6+ trick fails.

But Black overlooked **39 ♕xf5!**. It is the same ♗e7 mate after 39...♕xf5 or 39...exf5.

.

This came one move before the time control. The game ended with **39...♖g4 40 ♖h8+ ♔f7 41 ♕h7+ resigns.**

What was the final mistake? No, it wasn't 37...♕f4+??.

If Black had regained composure, instead of 39...♖g4?? he would have found 39...♕c1+! 40 ♔xc1 ♖g1+ 41 ♔d2 exf5 and tried to save the bishops of opposite color endgame.

Giving Back

The "How much is enough?" question often helps swindlers in another way. Their opponent can snuff out the swindler's tactical fire by returning some of the material won earlier. In this example, which decided a Candidates match, Black should have returned to approximate material equality before it was too late.

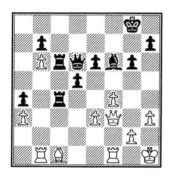

Korchnoi – Sax
Wijk aan Zee 1991

White to play

White's situation is grim: If Black gets to play 37...♖xb6, the a3-pawn is on life support. For example, 38 ♖xb6 ♕xb6 sets up ...♕b3 and ...♗xa3.

On 38 ♗d2 ♖b3! White must avoid creating a monster passed pawn, 38 ♖xb3? axb3 and ...b2. But 38 ♗b4 ♕d7 and ...♗e7 is also bad.

Since White cannot really stop 37...♖xb6, it made sense to look for kingside counterplay, such as 38 g4 and 39 f5.

He would have some chances after 38...♖xb6 39 ♖xb6 ♕xb6 40 f5!.

But instead of grabbing a pawn Black has 38...♖c2!. Then he may have the kingside attack, 38 f5?? ♕h2 mate or 38 ♕d1 d4! and ...♕d5+ (or 39 e4 ♖6c3!).

White bit the bullet with **37 ♗d2~**. This seems to violate one of a swindler's basic rules: Don't give your opponent an easier winning plan.

After **37...♕xa3** Black has a passed pawn and can win by pushing it because his bishop controls the queening square at a1.

White to play

White could safely resign if he allows 38...♕d3 39 ♖fd1 a3! and 40...a2!.

The point of his last move was **38 f5!**, threatening to capture on g6 or e6. He couldn't play this a move earlier because Black would simply capture with his e-pawn.

But with the queen diverted to a3, 38...exf5 allows 39 ♕xd5+. At least then he would have counterplay, e.g. 39...♔g7 40 ♕a5! with the idea of 41 ♗b4 ♕xe3 42 ♕a8!, threatening ♕f8 mate or ♕xb7+.

If White wins the b7-pawn, then his own b-pawn, supported by a rook becomes a powerful asset.

The absence of the black queen from d6 also meant that **38...gxf5 39 ♕g3+** was possible.

Black to play

The game can turn around with natural moves, 39...♗g7 40 ♕b8+ ♖c8 41 ♕xb7 and now 41...♕d3?? 42 ♕d7! and 43 b7 wins for White.

Even after 41...♕d6!, White gets the play he wants from 42 ♗b4 ♕c6 43 ♕e7!.

Black correctly saved his b-pawn with **39...♔f7!** and **40 ♕b8! ♕e7**.

White knew that he needed to keep finding forcing moves. Otherwise Black wins with ...a3-a2.

Even 41 g4, which would open another kingside line, can be ignored with 41...♖c8 42 ♕g3 a3, for example.

That meant the position demands **41 ♗b4!**. It is based on 41...♖xb4? 42 ♖xb4 ♕xb4 43 ♕xb7+ and ♕xc6.

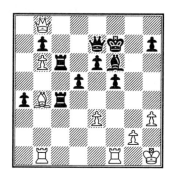

Black to play

This is when the crucial question becomes: "How much is enough?"

Black would win after 41...♖c8! and then 42 ♗xe7 ♖xb8 43 ♗d6 ♖a8. Or 42 ♕a7 ♕d7. After all, two extra pawns are two extra pawns.

The "enough" question is pertinent because White can improve with 42 ♕xc8! ♖xc8 43 ♗xe7 ♔xe7.

Then material is nearly equal. But the decisive factor is the Black bishop controls a1. That is, 44 ♖bc1 ♖xc1+ 45 ♖xc1 a3 and wins (46 ♖c2 ♗b2).

It takes longer after 44 ♖f2 ♖c3 or 44 ♖b5 ♖a8 but the outcome is the same: Black would win after 41...♖c8!.

But Black chose the computer-best **41...♕d7**. The major difference is that unlike 41...♖c8 this is not forcing.

White took advantage of his free hand with **42 ♕f8+ ♔g6 43 g4~**.

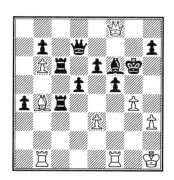

Black to play

He is still lost but at least he is trying. Computers prefer to prolong the agony with 43 ♕b8? or 43 ♕g8+? ♕g7 44 ♕e8+ ♕f7 45 ♕b8.

Instead, White has a threat, 44 ♕g8+, so that 44...♕g7? 45 gxf5+ exf5 46 ♖g1+ or 44...♔h6 45 g5+! ♗xg5 46 ♖g1.

Because he passed up a winning simplification (41...♖c8!) Black now had to calculate that move under more difficult circumstances (43...♖c8!).

It's more difficult because White can blow the kingside partially open. For example, 44 gxf5+ exf5 45 ♖g1+ wins for White after 45...♔h5?? 46 ♕xf6.

But it loses to 45...♖g4!. White's queen is attacked and 46 ♕d6 ♕xd6 47 ♗xd6 ♖xg1+ or 46 ♕xc8 ♕xc8 47 hxg4 fxg4 is doomed.

There was even a second win, besides 43...♖c8!. But it is less forcing and that makes it less trustworthy in time pressure, 43...♗g7 and 44 gxf5+ exf5 45 ♖g1+ ♔h6.

Black took the common-sense route of **43...f4**, a bid to keep the kingside file closed.

That would have won after **44 exf4** ...

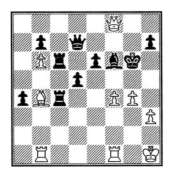

Black to play

... if Black had been able to calculate ...♖c8! one more time.

After 44...♖c8 White's queen has no good move so the only continuation to calculate was 45 f5+ exf5 46 gxf5+ and now 46...♕xf5!.

There are still some scary variations to check out, such as 47 ♖g1+ ♗g5 48 ♖xg5+ ♕xg5 49 ♕d6+ ♔h5! – not 49...♔g7?? 50 ♖g1 ♖c1 51 ♕e7+.

So much safer it seemed to play **44...♕d8??**.

The problem with that was **45 f5+ exf5 46 gxf5+ ♔h5 47 ♕f7+!**.

Now **47...♔h6** allows three different wins, 48 ♗f8+, 48 ♖g1 and the one White played, **48 ♗d2+ ♗g5 49 f6 resigns.**

Confuse Your Opponent

The skilled swindler knows that confusion on the board is his friend. When you are losing, your best chance can be creating a position that is difficult to calculate.

Short – Beliavsky
Barcelona 1989

White to play

In the previous three moves, White triggered tactics that seemed to lead to rough equality after he played 35 ♘xd8 ♖xd8. But now he saw that he would just be a knight down after 36...♘xd4.

With **35 e5!** he mobilized his one untapped resource, his center pawns.

Then 35...fxe5? 36 ♘xe5 would make the game a fight. For example, 36...♖xd6 37 ♘xc4 or 36...♘xd4 37 ♘xd7 are fairly even.

More complex is 36...♗b7 but then 37 d7! prepares ♘f7+.

Black kept his composure with **35...♕xc6!**. This should have won.

White to play

Computers recommend defeatist lines such as 36 ♖xc4 ♕b6+, although they concede that Black keeps his material after 37 ♔h2 fxe5.

But White's intention was to confuse his opponent with **36 e6~**.

This prompts Black to start thinking about those pawns, 36...♗b7?? 37 e7! and White wins.

79

Black can lose his big advantage after 36...♘xd4 37 ♕xd4 ♖xd6 38 e7! –
and then lose the game, 38...♖xd4?? 39 exd8(♕)+ and mates.

The position is getting chaotic and Black didn't notice how he could
neutralize the pawns with (36...♘xd4 37 ♕xd4) 37...♖b7!.

White would resign after, perhaps, 38 e7 ♖xe7! 39 dxe7 ♖xd4 40 ♖xd4
♔g8.

But it seemed safer to eliminate one of the pawns with **36...♖xd6**, a
perfectly good move.

White to play

There was only one realistic continuation, **37 e7**.

As positions become chaotic, players tend to rely more on intuition. It
made sense to block this pawn with a rook. But using a knight might have
been safer. That is, 37...♖b8 38 ♖xd6 ♘xd6 and ...♘e8.

That leaves his rook free, e.g. 39 ♕e6 ♕c5+ 40 ♔h1 ♘e8 41 ♕f7 h6 and
now 42 ♖d8 ♖b1+ mates.

But Black chose the more natural **37...♖e8 38 ♖xd6 ♘xd6**.

Once again White had only one tactical idea, the pinning **39 ♕e6!**.

Black had one good defense, **39...♕c5+ 40 ♔h1**.

Black to play

80

The e7-pawn is surprisingly more dangerous thanks to 37...♖e8. It looks like 40...♞c8 would kill the pawn but that it is a blunder that loses to 41 ♖d8.

Unfortunately for Black, he had other choices to consider. He could have tried 40...h6 and ...♔h7 and safeguard his king, for example.

Then 41 ♕xd6 ♕xd6 42 ♖xd6 ♖xe7 and then 43 ♖xa6 ♖c7 is a winning endgame.

But 41 ♖xd6! is at least equal (41...c3?? 42 ♖d8).

There is a forcing continuation, 40...♞f5, with ...♞xe7 in mind. Then 41 ♖d8 ♞g3+ leads to perpetual check, 42 ♔h2 ♞f1+ 43 ♔h1 ♞g3+.

But Black had reason to feel he was still winning. So he played **40...♞b7**, covering the d8 square. After **41 ♖d7**:

Black to play

The attacked knight cannot move (41...♞a5?? 42 ♖d8 and White wins).

Black tried for a good rook ending, **41...♕e5**, so that 42 ♕xe5 fxe5 43 ♖xb7 ♔g8 followed by ...♔f7 and ...♖xe7, with good winning chances.

But **42 ♕f7!** threatened to mate with ♕xe8 or ♕f8+.

A draw was agreed after **42...♖g8 43 ♖xb7 c3 44 ♖c7 ♕e1+**. White would win after 44...♕xc7?? 45 ♕xg8+.

Where did Black err? A better question is "Why did he err?"

The answer is that he was so focused on that super-hero e7-pawn that he forgot about his own passed pawn. He would have won easily after 40...c3! and 41...c2.

Even in the last diagram Black had winning chances if he had played 41...♕c8. He probably saw 42 ♕f7 ♕xd7 43 ♕f8+ loses. But he didn't see 42...c3!.

Then, for example, 43 ♖c7! ♕b8 44 ♖xc3? ♞d6 and 44 ♖xb7 c2 45 ♖c7! h6.

Stop Making Sense

Experienced players often survive tense tactical games by relying on common sense moves, especially when in time trouble. They don't over-think when they don't have enough time to think properly. But as the last example showed, if you can create enough chaos, common sense decisions can backfire:

Rowson – Emms
Gibraltar 2004

White to play

White is two pawns down and facing devastating pressure on b2 and c3. Black threatens 34...♖xb2+ 35 ♖xb2 ♖xb2+ 36 ♖xb2 ♘xc3+ 37 ♔a1 ♘b3+ mating.

Of course, 34 ♔a1 ♘b3 ┃ and 34 b3 ♖xb3+ is not salvation.

The computer-best 34 ♘xa4 and 34...♘xc2 35 ♖xc2 would prolong the game. That also sets a trap, 35...♖xa4?? 36 ♖c8+! ♔g7 37 ♖xb8 or 36...♖xc8?? 37 ♕xc8+ and 38 bxa3.

But with a modicum of caution, 35...♕xa4, the extra Exchange and two pawns would be more than enough for Black to win.

In mutual time pressure, White found an inspired bid to confuse, **34 ♘b5~**.

Black to play

It is confusing because all of Black's main options seem to win. In fact, they all do. "But visually there is a lot to process," White said after the game:

(a) 34...axb5 seems wrong because it closes the b-file. But after 35 ♖c8+ Black would win with 35...♖xc8 36 ♕xc8+ ♔g7. Or even 35...♔g7 (36 ♖xb8 ♘c3+).

(b) 34...♘xb5 also wins. But to play it Black has to be confident about 35 ♖c8+ ♖xc8 36 ♕xc8+ ♔g7 and then 37 ♖xf7+!.

That fails in complex variations such as 37...♔xf7 38 ♕d7+ ♔f6 39 ♕d8+ ♔e5! 40 ♕h8+ ♔xe4 41 ♗g2+ ♔e3.

(c) Similarly, 34...♖8xb5 35 ♖c8+ ♔g7 36 ♖xf7+ fails – but in time pressure it is hard to be sure.

(d) More pragmatic is 34...♖4xb5 35 ♗xb5 ♖xb5 although Black's material edge is reduced and he has to find moves after 36 ♕f4.

No human can analyze all that in time pressure. Black made the common-sense decision **34...♖xb2+ 35 ♖xb2 axb5**.

White to play

There was no reason to fear ♖c8+ now. Black will get the Exchange back with ...♘xb2 because that rook is more or less trapped. (36 ♖bd2 loses to 36...♘c3+)

Computers may tell you that 36 ♖b3 is best (36...♕xc1+ 37 ♔xc1 ♘xb3+ 38 axb3). But three extra pawns, going on four, make it an easy Black win.

The only recourse was, you guessed it, more confusion – **36 ♕f4~**.

It threatens 37 ♕xf7+ and 38 ♖h2 mate. And it seems to create new tactics, after 36...♖b7 37 ♕g5. (But 36...♖f8! would have won easily.)

Black preferred **36...♘c3+** and after **37 ♔a1** he had another choice.

Black to play

Again 37...♖f8 would have won. So would 37...♕a7. But common sense says Black should not be making his pieces passive when the tactics are reaching a peak.

They are actually pretty active after 37...♕a7 38 ♖h2 ♖a8! because he mates first after 39 ♕h6 ♘b3+! 40 ♖xb3 ♕xa2+!.

Black made the intuitive decision to keep his pieces more flexible with **37...♖b7**.

White still needed a miracle. He might have tried 38 ♕g5, with the idea of ♕d8+. But 38...♖d7 is more than adequate.

He changed the subject of the conversation with **38 ♕e3~**. That gave Black something new to think about, the threat to his knight.

(It set a delicious trap 38...♘c6 39 ♖fc2! b4 40 ♖xc3! and wins).

Black to play

An appropriate end of the game would have been 38...♕c5 (threatening to win the queen with 39...♘b3+) and 39 ♕h6 ♘b3+! 40 ♖xb3 ♕xf2 White resigns.

But Black answered with a common sense move, **38...e5??**. Neither player understood how bad this was – even when White annotated the game for *New in Chess* magazine.

It is bad because 39 ♗c4! defends the key a2 and b3 squares. Since that kills Black's best tactical ideas, White would be poised to mate with ♖h2 and ♕h6. Chances are equal after 39...♕a8 40 ♗xf7+.

But White tried **39 ♕g5?**, threatening 40 ♕d8+.

Black passed up 39...♕a5 and set a trap of his own **39...♖a7**. Play went **40 ♕d8+ ♔g7 41 ♕f6+ ♔g8**.

White to play

White has perpetual check. Should he try for more with 42 ♖h2, threatening mate on h8?

No, that allows a tactic we saw earlier, 42...♘b3+! 43 ♖xb3 ♕xa2+! 44 ♖xa2 ♖xa2 mate.

He found **42 ♗c4!**. Once again his king is safeguarded against ...♘b3+. There is no reprieve in 42...bxc4 43 ♖b8+ and mates.

Black played **42...d5** and **resigned** after **43 ♖h2!**.

It is easy to blame 39...♖a7??. It was the losing move. But swindling is a process, as we'll see in Chapter Eight. The process in this game began when Black chose common-sense moves in situations (moves 34, 37, 38) when he needed to calculate.

Going Crazy

When all else fails, chaos can be induced by moves that look ludicrous. Your opponent may wonder if you've gone crazy. You shouldn't care.

If you are going to lose with sane moves, try the alternative. Here's a memorable example:

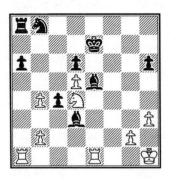

V. Georgiev – Fernandes
Elgoibar 1998

White to play

The game has already been pretty wild, as the position indicates. Black's bishops give him the edge and he threatens 30...♔d7 31 ♘-moves ♗xb2, for example.

White can minimize his disadvantage with 30 ♘f3. After 30...♘d7 31 ♖a5 he would prepare 32 b5.

He might draw despite the very weak b2- and d5-pawns after 31...♖b8 32 ♖xa6 ♖xb4 33 ♖a7.

But he overestimated the value of the passed pawn he created with **30 ♘c6+? ♘xc6 31 dxc6.**

He threatened 32 b5, when 32...a5?? 33 b6 and the pawns win. This is the kind of finish that remains in the minds of both players for several moves, a dream for White, a nightmare for Black.

But Black found what should have been the decisive moves of the game, **31...♔d8! 32 b5 a5.**

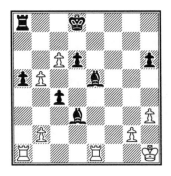

White to play

White has made matters worse. The computer-best 33 b6 contains a not-so-obvious threat of 34 ♖f1! and ♖f8+.

For example, 34 ♖f1! ♗xf1 35 ♖xf1 ♔e7 36 b7 ♖b8 37 c7 is a version of the Black nightmare. (Or 35...♗g7 36 ♖f7.)

But Black can neutralize the pawns with 33...♖a6! 34 b7 ♔c7 followed by ...♖b6 and ...♔xc6.

This told White it was time to go desperate. He rolled the dice with **33 b4~**.

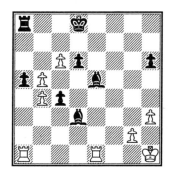

Black to play

It's a crazy move, of course. Even if he got to capture on a5 it wouldn't be nearly enough to save the game.

Black can play 33...♔c7 so that 34 ♖xa5 ♖xa5 35 bxa5 c3! and ...♗xb5 wins.

If White is desperate enough for 33 b4 he would meet 33...♔c7 with 34 bxa5~. Then on 34...♗xa1 he queens following 35 ♖e7+ ♔d8 36 ♖d7+ ♔e8 67 b6.

(Unfortunately, he gets mated first, after 67...♖xa5 68 b7 ♖b5 69 c7 ♖b1+ 70 ♔h2 ♗e5+.)

But Black wanted to make it easier, with **33...♗xa1!**. Then 34 ♖xa1 ♔c7 35 bxa5 c3 and again ...♗xb5.

Therefore **34 b6~** was the only realistic try. White threatens the nightmare finish 35 c7+ ♔d7 36 b7. Or 35...♔c8 36 ♖e8+.

Black to play

87

Black cannot play 34...♖a6 because of 35 c7+ ♔d7 36 ♖e8! wins.

But plugging up the e-file with **34...♗e5!** was sufficient.

After 35 b7 ♖b8 36 bxa5 Black finishes off with 35...♔c7, 35...c3 or even 35...♗d4 36 ♖e8+ ♔c7!. Almost any move should win. After all he has the two-bishop advantage, literally.

But the unwritten rule of chaotic positions is that they often reward one bizarre move after another. White's was **35 b5~**.

If Black had realized that this makes a threat, he would have looked for his own strange moves. He is so far ahead in material that 35...♖b8! works.

It threatens ...♖xb6 and allows 36 c7+ ♔c8 37 cxb8(♕)+ ♔xb8. Then White's queenside pawns are harmless but Black's (...a4-a3) would win swiftly.

There is an even stranger defense, 35...♗f5, so that 36 ♖f1 ♗c8!.

However, Black played the natural **35...c3?** and **36 b7 ♖b8 37 b6**.

Suddenly he was lost (38 c7+). He played **37...d5** and **resigned** before 38 ♖xe5.

The rule of chaotic positions applied until the end. Another bizarre move, 36...♖c8!, would have won. For example, 37 bxc8(♕)+ ♔xc8 38 b6 c2.

A true swindler, however, would keep going with 37 b6. Then only one move wins and Black would have to find it, 37...c2! so that 38 c7+ ♖xc7! 39 b8(♕)+ ♖c8 40 ♕a7 c1(♕).

Quiz

11.

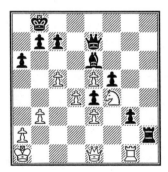

Krasenkow – Dolmatov
Moscow 1989

Black to play

The g3-pawn is lost and future endgames look bad because of the superior white knight. What should Black do?

12.

Glek – Lazarev
Porto San Giorgio 1997

White to play

Which is better, 42 ♕xd5 or 42 ♖c8, which threatens 43 ♗c5?

Chapter Five:
The Swindlee

Why does someone fall for a swindle? Let's step into the mind of a swindle victim and see. We will find several reasons.

(1) *The swindlee believes only two results are possible.*

Those two results are a win for him and a draw. His advantage is so great that it blinds him to the possibility of the third result.

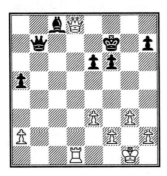

Filip – Darga
Oberhausen 1961

White to play

White can add to his huge advantage with 29 ♖c1 because 29...♗d7 30 ♖c7 wins the bishop.

Black would have nothing left but a desperate lunge for perpetual check, 30...♕b1+ 31 ♔g2 ♕e4+.

There are various ways to stop the checks but the simplest is 32 f3!. Black would almost certainly resign then.

It was hard to explain **29 h4?** or **29...♕f3 30 ♖c1?** except by time trouble.

Then **30...♗b7** allowed Black to dream of mate on g2 or h1.

Both players must have expected that White would be delivering mate in the next few moves. But after **31 ♖c7+ ♔g6 32 ♕g8+ ♔f5** the black king was safe.

White to play

White's miscues prolonged the game. But he could still win a queen endgame after, for example, 33 ♖c5+ ♗d5 34 ♖xd5+ and 35 ♕xh7+.

Incredibly, the game ended with **33 ♕xh7+?? ♔g4** and White **resigned**.

He had counted on 35 ♖xb7 but then saw that 35...♔h3! mates.

The greater the expectation of victory, the more remote seems the possibility of defeat. That eternal truth also cost White in this endgame.

Dzadnidze – Rajlich
St. Petersburg 2009

White to play

Half of endgame textbooks seem to be devoted to rook endings in which one player has an extra pawn. Subtle differences determine whether or not the defender can draw. But:

50 ♔g1 ♔g3 51 ♔f1 g4 52 d7 ♖f2+ 53 ♔e1 ♖f7! 54 ♔e2 ♔xg2 55 ♔e3 g3 56 ♔e4 ♔f2 57 ♔e5 g2 58 ♔e6 ♖xd7 59 ♖xd7 g1(♕) and Black won.

What were White's mistakes? It must have taken several to lose, didn't it?

No, her only major error was **53 ♔e1??**. After 53 ♔g1! ♖xg2+ 54 ♔f1! the game should be drawn.

But she lost for another reason: White was thinking of those textbook positions and saying to herself: This is going to be either a win or a draw. How do I make it a win?

The reality is that with the best moves for White and Black the position in the diagram was a draw. Black's king and rook were too well placed.

That was a case of one-player luck. Black didn't do much to induce a blunder. Winning a pawn-down endgame requires more skill. But it is based on concealing the possibility of a third result. Here is an example of a two-pawn-down swindle.

Sevian – van Wely
Monzon 2016

White to play

This seems certain to simplify into a battle between White's king, rook and two pawns against Black's king and rook. In some cases a book draw is possible. But a book win is more likely.

After **48 ♖b5+**, Black, a crafty veteran grandmaster, had two legal moves and the correct one seemed obvious.

But if he had played 48...♔a3, his young opponent would see that 49...♔xa2 was threatened.

That would tell White that there was a chance for him to lose. For example, 49 c5 ♔xa2 50 b4 a3 51 ♖b6 ♖f8 42 c6 ♔b2 and now 53 c7?? ♖c8 54 ♖b7 a2 and Black wins.

Seeing that, White would probably eliminate the dangerous a- pawn with 50 bxa4. The game would be drawn after Black played 50...♔xa4 or 50...♔xa2.

Black's **48...♔c3~** seemed to risk losing because there is no immediate threat of ...♔xa2.

There may even be positions ahead in which White queens the c-pawn with check. White played **49 c5**.

Black to play

Now 49...♔b2 would threaten the a2-pawn one move later than 48...♔a3 would.

Is that significant? Yes, 49...♔b2 50 bxa4+ ♔xa2 51 ♖b6 or 51 a5 turns out to be a winning version of a ♔+♖+2♙s -vs.- ♔+♖ ending.

Black's devious idea was revealed by **49...a3!**. It was time for White to realize that ...♔b2xa2 would make possible a third result, a loss.

After **50 ♖b6 ♖f8** he could have saved his a2-pawn with 51 ♖e6 and ♖e2+.

The game would be drawn after 51...♖c8 52 c6 ♔b2 53 ♖e2+ ♔c3 and ...♖xc6, for example.

But why retreat the rook when you have winning chances? White pressed on with **51 b4 ♔b2**.

White to play

Let's stop calculating for a moment and think in general terms:

We can see that ...♔xa2 cannot be stopped. Then Black will be three moves away from queening. White's king is cut off from the queenside. Can his rook alone promote a pawn before Black does?

That doesn't seem possible and this is confirmed by variations such as 52 c6 ♔xa2 53 c7?? ♖c8. White loses after 54 ♖b7 ♔b2 and ...a2.

There was no simple way to force a draw, as there was with 51 ♖e6 and ♖e2+. But there were ways for White to play for a win after **52 b5 ♔xa2.**

He could have set a trap with 53 c6. That would win after 53...♔b2 54 ♖a6 a2?? 55 b6!. For example, 55...a1(♕) 56 ♖xa1 ♔xa1 and both 57 c7 and 57 b7 win.

But 53 c6 allows Black to draw by eliminating pawns, 53...♔b3 54 ♖a6 ♔b4 55 b6 ♔b5! (56 ♖xa3 ♔xb6).

White to play

Instead, White set a different trap with **53 ♖a6!**.

Then 53...♔b2?? 54 b6! a2 55 c6 transposes into the 53 c6 ♔b2 54 ♖a6 win.

This trap is deeper than the one that 53 c6 would have set. This time 53...♔b3?? also loses, to 54 b6!. For example, 54...♔b4 55 b7! ♔xc5 56 ♖a8 or 57...♖b8 58 c6.

But Black alertly found **53...♖f5!**.

This is the last point at which all three results are possible. Clearly 54 b6? ♖xc5 is wrong, since Black would be winning with ...♔b3 or ...♔b2 and ...a2.

White to play

94

But White has the superior 54 c6!. This looks very similar to 54 b6 ♖xc5. The difference is that 54 c6 ♖xc5 55 ♔f4 gets the king to the queenside in time.

For example, 55...♔b2 56 ♔e4 a2 57 ♔d4 a1(♕) 58 ♖xa1 ♔xa1 59 c7.

Black would be the one in danger of losing. He needs to find 59...♖b4+ 60 ♔c5 ♖b1! or 60 ♔d5 ♖d5+ 61 ♔d6 ♖b6+ 62 ♔d7 ♖b7!.

But White apparently didn't want to give up his last winning chance. After **54 ♖c6??** he managed to queen with check, **54...♔b2 55 b6 a2 56 b7 a1(♕) 57 b8(♕)+.**

Black to play

However, even with an extra pawn, he was lost because his king was much more vulnerable than Black's. The end was **57...♔c2 58 ♔g4 ♖f2 59 ♕g3 ♕g7+ 60 ♔h3 ♕h7+ 61 ♔g4 ♕f5+ 62 ♔h4 ♖f4+ White resigns**.

And, incidentally, the initial position was only a draw with best play (48 ♖d3 ♖f1 and ...♖a1, for example.)

These examples show how overconfidence can fuel a swindle. A different failing is haste:

(2) *The swindlee wants to win quickly.*

Well, don't we all? But one of the weapons that a would-be swindler can wield is the threat to drag out a game.

Volokitin – Movsesian
Russian Team
Championship 2008

Black to play

95

After 61...♕xb3, White would capture on a5. That creates a ♔+♕ -vs.- ♔+♖ endgame. Beginners learn that that is a book win for the player with the queen. Tablebases tell us that with best play Black can deliver checkmate in 20 moves after 62 ♔xa5, for example.

What beginners are *not* taught, by books or tablebases, is that to find the best moves Black will need a lot of knowledge, experience or calculation.

He wanted to spare himself an hour or two. He looked for away to pick off the rook and found **61...♕d6+**. It works after 62 ♔xa5 ♕d2+! and 62 ♔a7 ♕e7+!.

This was a no-risk trap for Black because after **62 ♔b5!** he could have gone back to the book win with 62...♕b4+ and 63...♕xb3.

Instead, he quickly played **62...♕d3+ 63 ♔a4! ♕e4+? 64 ♔xa5** because he had visualized a winning fork, 64...♕e1+. It was an optical illusion.

Black to play

Black's bid to shorten the game has prolonged it. With best play, it will take Black nearly 40 moves to deliver mate now.

After some more inexact moves, **64...♕a8+? 65 ♔b4 ♕f8+? 66 ♖c5!**, he had allowed White to coordinate his forces. His king can protect his pawn and his rook. The rook can also be protected by the pawn in some cases.

After **66...♔d6 67 ♖c4 ♔d5+ 68 ♔c3 ♕a3 69 ♔c2 ♕a2+ 70 ♔c3 ♕b1 71 ♖d4+ ♔e5 72 ♖c4 ♕c1+ 73 ♔b4 ♕b2 74 ♔a4 ♔d5 75 ♔b4 ♕a1 76 ♖c5+ ♔d4 77 ♖c4+ ♔d3 78 ♔b5 ♕a7 79 ♔b4 ♕e7+ 80 ♔b5** Black was still nearly 40 moves away from forcing mate.

And after **80...♕a3?? 81 b4!** it was no longer a win. Black played another 63 moves before conceding a draw.

Black was not wrong to try to win quickly back at the first diagram. But the forced win was hard to find, 61...a4! 62 bxa4 ♕d6+! 63 ♔b5 ♕d3+and the rook falls (64 ♔b6 ♕e3+ or 64 ♔c6 ♕d7+ 65 ♔c5 ♕e7+).

This was not a swindle. White did not have to do anything tricky. It is in middlegames that there are many more opportunities for an alert defender to swindle a hasty opponent.

Khenkin – Timman
Malmo 2006

White to play

White saw that 33 ♕d4 would force queens off the board (since 33...♕e6?? or 33...♕b3?? hangs the rook, 34 ♕xc5).

After 33 ♕d4 ♕xd4 34 ♖xd4 ♖e5 35 b4 White would have excellent winning chances as he brings his king to the queenside.

If he can also swap rooks, his winning chances increase. For instance, 33 ♕d4 h5 34 ♕xc4 ♖xc4 35 ♖d4! ♖xd4? 36 exd4 ♔g6 and Black will soon run out of good moves after 37 ♔f1 ♔f5 38 ♔e2 and ♔e3.

There's a third possible endgame, with just rooks. For example, 35...♖c5 36 ♘xe4 ♘xe4 37 ♖xe4 ♖c1+ 38 ♔h2 ♖c2 38 ♖f4 also leaves White with strong winning chances.

But take another look at the diagram. You can see that White's pieces are more active than Black's. Shouldn't he be able to finish the game faster? He tried **33 ♕b8**.

Black asked himself whether 34 ♖h8+ was a threat he must avert. When he saw it wasn't (34...♔g6 35 ♕g3+ ♖g5) he replied **33...♖a5!**.

White to play

Black may have his own last-rank threats after ...♖a1+ and ...♕f1.

White can set a trap with 34 ♔h2 so that ...♖a1 will not be a check. He would win after 34...♖a1? 35 ♖h8+ ♔g6 36 ♕g3+ and 37 ♕xg7.

But Black can temporize with 34...♖f5 and put the burden on White.

White can set a different trap with 34 ♕f4. It threatens to win the e4-pawn with 35 ♖d4. He would win quickly after 34...♖a1+? 35 ♔h2 ♕f1 35 ♕f5+ g6 36 ♕xf6.

But again Black can resist, with 34...♕b4 (35 ♖d4 ♕xb2).

White's feeling that he was close to a knockout led to **34 ♖c8** so that, say, 34...♕e6? 35 ♘e2! sets up a fork, 36 ♖h8+ ♔g6 37 ♘f4+.

He would win after 35...♕e5 36 ♖h8+ ♔g6 37 ♘f4+ ♔g5 38 ♕f8!.

But 34 ♖c8?? was shown to be an error by **34...♖a1+ 35 ♔h2 ♕f1!**.

White to play

What should have been a methodical endgame grind for White (after 33 ♕d4!) has turned into a calculating contest.

Black has the greater threats, beginning with 36...♕g1+ 37 ♔g3 ♘h5 ! and mates (38 ♔g4 ♕xf2). He also threatens 36...♕h1+ 37 ♔g3 ♖g1!.

White may have foreseen this position when he chose 34 ♖c8 and assumed that he must be better because gets to check first.

But after **36 ♖h8+ ♔g6 37 ♕g3+ ♔f5** he had no effective follow-up. After **38 ♕f4+** Black hesitated with **38...♔g6**.

But White had nothing better than to repeat the position, **39 ♕g3+ ♔f5 40 ♕f4+**, since 40 ♕h4 ♕h1+ 41 ♔g3 g5 42 ♕xh6 ♖g1 is death.

Black found **40...♔e6!** and White had run out of free checks.

White to play

The only question now was whether Black could avoid perpetual check after **41 ♖e8+ ♘xe8 42 ♕xe4+**.

The answer was **42...♔d7 43 ♕f5+ ♔e7 44 ♕c5+ ♘d6 45 e4 ♕c4** and White soon **resigned**. Or 45 ♘e4 ♕d1 and 45 ♘d5+ ♔e6 46 ♕c6 ♕d1.

Neither player was likely to see all that, or even a fraction of it, when the position after 34 ♖c8 arose. But if White had looked at the board from Black's point of view he might have realized the dangers. That also explains a third reason why a player allows himself to be swindled:

(3) *He focuses on his own tactics.*

When a player has outplayed his opponent tactically he has reason to expect that this will continue. He can conclude that either he is simply a better tactician or that his opponent was having a bad day.

Zukertort – Steinitz
London 1883

White to play

It seems as if White just had to avoid 29 ♖xf4?? ♕e1+ to win.

The passive 29 ♖g1 would bring him closer to victory after 29...♕xb2 30 ♖b3!, when Black's king is suddenly vulnerable.

For instance, 30...♕xc2 31 ♖xb7 ♕xa2?? loses outright to 32 ♖e1+.

But 29...♘c5 is not so clear, after 30 ♕xa7 ♕xb2. And 30 b3? ♘e4 sets up a smothered mate on f2.

So, White chose **29 ♖e1+!**. He was looking for tactics such as 29...♔f6?? 30 ♕h8+. For example, 30...♔f5 31 ♕c8! and wins.

Black could have tried 29...♘e5 because 30 ♕xb7+?! ♔f6 leaves White with problems. But he would still be dealing with a two-result position.

Instead, Black replied **29...♖e4!**.

White to play

It didn't seem logical to play 30 ♖g1 a move after rejecting 29 ♖g1. But with 30 ♖g1! there is no longer a smothered mate threat of ...♘e4-f2.

And with Black's rook is off the f-file, White has his own mating ideas. For example, 30...♘c5 31 ♖h8! is strong.

Then 31...♕xb2? 32 ♕e8+ ♔f6 and 33 ♖f1+! ♔g5 34 ♕d8+ wins.

However, White appeared so certain of victory that the game went **30 ♖xe4+ ♕xe4 31 ♕xa7**.

The queen defends against the last-rank mate (31...♕e1+ 32 ♕g1).

White must have assumed that with one pair of rooks gone, the win would be easier because Black can't block checks as easily. He may have counted on winning after 31...♕xc2 32 ♖e3+. He was wrong about that but...

Black to play

The greater problem was **31...b6!**. The only way to avert ...♕e1 mate is the hopeless 32 ♖e3 ♕xe3 33 h3. White **resigned.**

It wasn't just that he overlooked 31...b6. White would also have been lost after 31...♘c5 32 ♕a5 ♕e2!. That's an indication that he lost with 30 ♖xe4+?? because he wasn't considering his opponent's most basic tactical idea.

As we said in Chapter One, luck is fickle. The player who finds several brilliant moves can find his work undone by overlooking a single good one by the opponent. Here's a dramatic example.

Lputian – H. Olafsson
Debrecen 1992

White to play

After a sharp opening White played **21 ♘xb8**.

He must have expected 21...♗xg2 22 ♔xg2 ♕b7+ followed by ...♗xb8 and perhaps ...♕c7, with rough equality.

Instead Black unveiled the stunning **21...♗e3!!**. He threatened to win with 22...♕g3.

White would have to give up gobs of material after 22 fxe3? ♕g3.

For example, 23 ♖d5 exd5 or 23 e4 ♗xe4 24 ♕xe4 ♘xe4.

And he would get mated after 22 ♗xb7? ♕g3+ (23 ♗g2 ♗xf2+ 24 ♔h1 ♘g4! and 24 ♔f1 ♗e3).

White to play

How desperate should White be? There are no swindle ideas for him. He could try 22 ♔h1 so that 22...♗xf2! 23 ♕d3 allows him to protect key squares at g3 and h3.

But after Black recaptures on b8 he will have two pawns for the Exchange in a position that is still very double-edged.

White found **22 ♕b3!** and some computers at first consider it a winning move. Black would run out of ammunition following 22...♕g3 23 ♕xb7! ♗xf2+ 24 ♔f1! ♗e3 25 ♕f3.

Black could have played on with 24...♘d5! rather than 24...♗e3. That would win after 25 exd5?? ♗e3.

But White would be better after 25 ♖xd5! ♗e3 26 ♖f5 or 25...exd5 26 ♕xd5 ♗d4 27 ♕f3.

However, this tactical battle was just beginning. Black replied **22...♘g4!**.

White to play

It was White's turn to be declared dead by computers – and this time the machines were right.

He would be mated after 23 hxg4 ♕g3 24 ♕xb7 ♕xf2+ (25 ♔h1 ♕h4+).

He could resign after 24 ♖d5 ♗xf2+ and 25...♗e3.

There was on possible escape route, **23 ♕xb7 ♕h2+ 24 ♔f1**. White is ahead so much material he could win after 24...♗xf2 25 e3!.

For instance, 25...♘xe3+ 26 ♔xf2 ♘xd1+ 27 ♖xd1 ♖xb8 28 ♕xa7 or 28 ♕e7.

Black was not done: **24...♘xf2!** threatened 25...♘xd1 (or 25...♘d3) and 26...♕g1 mate.

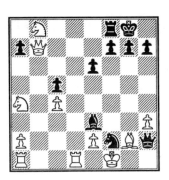

White to play

There was only one way to keep the game going in a meaningful manner.

It was **25 ♕f3! ♘xd1 26 ♔e1!**. The would-be swindler searches for ways of denying the opponent an easy victory, even when it seems fruitless.

White would be alive after 26...♕g1+ 27 ♕f1, when Black's best is to repeat the position (27...♕h2 28 ♕f3).

Better is 26...♗f2+ 27 ♔xd1 ♕g1+ 28 ♔c2 ♕xa1, with a moderate Black advantage. But Black felt, correctly, that there should be a forcing way to win.

It was very difficult to see that the retreat 26...♕xb8! would threaten 27...♕b4+, e.g. 27 ♔xd1 ♖d8+ 28 ♔e1 ♕b4+ 29 ♔f1 ♗d4 and wins.

Black felt he had a simpler win with **26...♖d8** and 27...♗f2+.

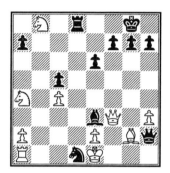

White to play

Black has been having a great game. He found some wonderful shots, 21...♗e3!!, 22...♘g4! and 24...♘xf2!. He had reason to feel he *should* win.

But a good swindler is always alert to exploit "shoulds." White found the only move, **27 ♘d7!**. It is based on 27...♖xd7 28 ♕a8+.

Black could retain a sizable edge 27...♕g1+ since 28 ♗f1 ♗f2+ 29 ♔xd1 ♕xf1+ 30 ♔c2 ♕xa1 wins.

Play could go 28 ♕f1 ♕xf1+ 29 ♗xf1 ♖xd7 30 ♖xd1 ♗f2+ and 28...♗d2+ 29 ♔xd1! ♕d4!.

But the shock of 27 ♘d7! had its residual effect: **27...♗f2+? 28 ♔xd1 ♕g1+ 29 ♔c2 ♕xa1 30 ♕xf2 ♖xd7?** (30...♕xa2+ first) **31 ♘c3** and White consolidated and won.

(4) The swindlee expects to make steady progress.

When a player squeezes an advantage out of a roughly even middlegame, he may be expecting his position to keep improving. That means finding moves that make visible progress – advances of pieces or pawns, favorable exchanges, and the like. But visible progress is often deceptive.

Anand – Kasparov
New York 1994

White to play

White has good reason to think he might win. He has an extra pawn and a promising plan of pushing h4-h5. Black has had nothing better to do than moving his rook up and down the a-file for several moves.

How should White proceed? He could try ♘e2 and ♘c1 to protect the a-pawn and then attack the c5-pawn with ♘b3.

His h-pawn can become strong, e.g. 43 ♘e2 ♖ga8 44 h5! and 45...♖xa2? 46 ♖xa2 ♖xa2 47 h6 ♖a8 and now 48 ♘c1 followed by ♘b3xc5.

This looks doubtful after 48...♗a4. But the pinning 49 ♖a2! would have won.

Instead, White hit upon a different idea, getting his knight to e4. Play went **43 ♘h3 ♗e4 44 ♘f2 ♗c6 45 ♔f4 ♖ga8**.

White to play

Now 46 ♘e4 would likely prompt 46...♗xe4 47 ♔xe4. This gains White a free hand for h4-h5.

Computers claim a solid advantage for him. But after 47...♔f8! and ...♔g7 they cannot make progress, even if White gets his protected, passed pawn to h6.

That was an upsetting revelation. White seemed to be getting closer to a win with his last moves. The logic of chess suggested he should be able to keep making progress.

That's what apparently led him to play **46 h5?** and then **46...♖xa2 47 ♖xa2 ♖xa2 48 h6**.

The h-pawn was stopped by **48...♖a8** in view of 49 h7 ♖h8.

The position is roughly balanced and there was certainly no reason for Black to win. Nevertheless, White lost his way, **49 ♘d1 ♔f8 50 ♘b2? ♔g8 51 ♔g3 ♖a1**.

The rest was played inexactly but White eventually resigned, soon after **52 ♖f2 ♗e8 53 ♖e2 ♖g1+ 54 ♔h4 ♗c6 55 ♖f2 ♖e1 56 h7+ ♔h8 57 ♖xf7 ♖e3! 58 ♘d1 ♖xd3**.

"Making progress" can be a psychological weapon for the player with advantage. As his position improves, his opponent may become depressed. But progress is a double-edged sword:

When Kasparov held a two-pawn advantage in an endgame of the 1993 world championship match he and his opponent, Nigel Short, made their moves quickly, "out of inertia," as Kasparov put it. He expected Short to resign as soon as Kasparov's pawns were advanced far enough. So he made a "gruesome mistake" by pushing a pawn too quickly. But it was the next-to-last mistake. Short counter-blundered and lost.

Humans are burdened by the belief that advances (46 h5? and 48 h6 in the last game) should be better than retreats (43 ♘e2! and ♘c1). We think that progress means going forward.

But in a middlegame, pieces that advance can turn out to be over-extended. That's another opportunity for the would-be swindler.

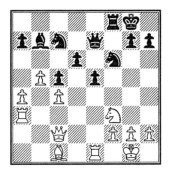

Seirawan – I. Ivanov
Los Angeles 1991

White to play

White has a material as well as a positional edge. Experience tells him he isn't far from a winning position.

How does he get there? Computer recommendations such as 25 ♕d1, 25 a5 and 25 ♘g5 h6 26 ♘h3 are hardly convincing.

White hit on **25 ♘h4**. He can attack on the kingside with ♘f5/♖g3.

After 25...g6, he can target g6 with another advance 26 ♗h6. He would have a winning endgame after 26...♖f7 27 ♘xg6! hxg6 28 ♕xg6+ ♖g7 29 ♕xg7+ ♕xg7 30 ♗xg7 ♔xg7, e.g. 31 a5 or 31 ♖d3.

Play went **25...♘e6 26 ♘f5 ♕d7.**

White seems to have made progress since the diagram and can inch closer to victory after, for example, 27 a5 or 27 f3 (to take e4 away from Black's minor pieces).

White to play

But White expected more evident progress. That suggests 27 ♕d3. After Black defends his d6-pawn with 27...♘d4 28 ♘xd4 exd4, for example, White can dominate the open file with 29 ♖a2 and ♖ae2.

He went for kingside attack with **27 ♖h3 g6 28 ♘h6+ ♔g7 29 f3**.

But White's kingside pieces aren't threatening anything. In fact, they are over-extended and potentially vulnerable.

After **29...♘d4 30 ♕d3 ♘h5!** Black was making his first serious threats of the game.

He could even be brilliant, if 31...♕xh3! 32 gxh3 ♘xf3+ with at least a draw was allowed.

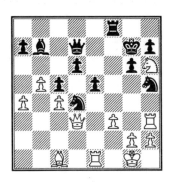

White to play

The best way to foil that was 31 ♘g4. After 31...♘f4 32 ♗xf4 exf4 White should be close to winning. But with his rook out of play on h3, that didn't *look* like winning.

White chose **31 ♖f1**, which at least ruled out sacrifices on f3 and h3. He didn't realize his advantage was disappearing.

Black might have tried 31...♖f4 so that he threatened 32...♔xh6. He would be winning after 32 ♗xf4? ♘xf4 33 ♕e3 ♘xh3+.

But when an opponent is floundering, a swindler knows not to allow him to calculate his way to a clearer position (31...♖f4 32 ♖xh5! gxh5 33 ♗xf4 exf4 34 ♕d2 ♔xh6 35 ♕xf4+).

Black correctly preferred **31...♘f4! 32 ♗xf4 ♖xf4**.

Now White had to worry about threats to his kingside pieces with ...♗c8/...♕d8.

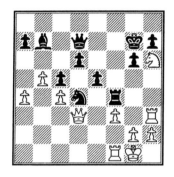

White to play

After **33 ♘g4?** there was one good move and Black found it, **33...e4!**.

Then 34 fxe4 ♕xg4 35 ♖xf4 ♕xf4 is bad and 35...♘e2+! and 36...♘xf4 is worse.

White's **34 ♕e3** granted Black a nice 34...exf3! and then 35 ♕xf4 ♘e2+ 36 ♔f2 ♘xf4. (That should win even after 37 ♖xh7+! ♔xh7 38 ♘f6+ ♔g7 39 ♘xd7 fxg2).

Time pressure was evident in **34...h5 35 ♘f2 exf3 36 g3?**.

White needed to hold tight with 36 ♖e1 and try to catch a breather by reaching move 40, when he could study the position at length.

Black to play

The game's final error permitted Black to end with a swindler's dream combination, **36...♞e2+ 37 ♚h1 ♛xh3!**.

It would be mate after 38 ♞xh3 f2+ and a lost endgame after 38 ♛e7+ ♜f7 39 ♞xh3 ♜xe7.

Instead, it was **38 ♜g1 ♛g2+! White resigns.**

(5) The swindlee goes "swimming."

"Swimming" is a term that describes a player's behavior when he is convinced that routine moves are good enough to win his advantageous position. Sometimes this policy works. But with several pieces on the board something more is often required.

Keres – Geller
Moscow 1962

1 d4 ♞f6 2 c4 c5 3 d5 e5 4 ♞c3 d6 5 g3 g6 6 ♝h3 ♞bd7 7 ♞f3 a6 8 0-0 ♝g7 9 e4 0-0 10 ♜e1 ♞e8 11 ♛d3 ♞c7 12 ♝g5 f6 13 ♝d2 ♜b8 14 a4 b6 15 ♞h4 ♚h8 16 ♛f1 ♜f7? 17 ♝e6!

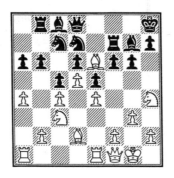

Black to play

This wins the Exchange since 17...♘xe6? 18 dxe6 and 17...♖f8?? 18 ♘xg6+! hxg6 19 ♕h3+ are worse.

17...♕e7 18 ♕h3 ♔g8 19 f4! exf4 20 gxf4 ♕e8 21 ♗xf7+ ♕xf7 22 ♕g3 ♘e8 23 ♖e2! ♕e7 24 ♖ae1 ♘c7

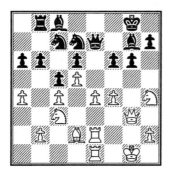

White to play

25 ♘f3 ♗b7

White could have probably shortened the game with 25 e5! fxe5 26 ♘e4 and 26...♘f6 27 ♘xd6! or 26...♘e8 27 f5!.

But he has been making so much progress, there was no reason to take risks. He could have chosen a low-risk option (after 25 ♘f3 ♗b7) of kingside attack with 26 h4! and 27 h5. That idea remains an option for several moves.

26 ♘d1 b5 27 ♗a5 ♘e8 28 axb5 axb5 29 cxb5 ♖a8 30 ♗d2 ♖a4 31 ♘h4 ♘c7

He has been able to steadily improve his position with solid moves. Moreover, these moves did not require him to calculate more than one move or two moves ahead.

White to play

But now that his pieces are at their peak of coordination it was a good time to calculate further. One of the possible knockout blows was 32 ♘f5. Black could not last long after 32...♕f8 33 ♘xg7 followed by ♘c3 and ♖g2, for example.

That means 32 ♘f5! gxf5 33 exf5 ♛f8 34 ♖e7 would be crucial. Had White examined this he would have seen that he would regain his piece favorably (34...♗c8 35 b6!). The game would be drawing to a close.

After **32 ♛b3? ♘b6 33 ♘f3? ♛d7!** White was swimming.

Black's heavy pieces were becoming more active, e.g. 34 ♘c3 ♖b4 35 ♛c2 ♛g4+ 36 ♔f2 ♛h5.

He would be ready to awaken his sleeping minor pieces with 37...f5!.

Then 38 exf5 ♗d4+ 39 ♘xd4 ♛xh2+ allows perpetual check and 39 ♔g3 ♘bxd5! could lead to any of the three results.

White to play

Since ...f5 and ...♛g4+ have become possible, it was suggested after the game that 34 f5 gxf5 35 ♘c3 was right.

White would seize the initiative after 35...♖b4 36 ♛c2. For example, 36...♘xb5 37 ♖g2 with a threat of ♗h6. Or 36...fxe4 37 ♘xe4 ♖c4 38 ♗c3!.

But White continued what seemed like a safety-first policy, **34 ♖g2?**. He felt he could wait a move for a 35 f5 that required less calculation.

He wasn't allowed to – **34...f5!** equalized chances.

For example, 35 exf5 ♗xd5 36 ♛d3 ♗d4+ and 37...♛xb5. Worse is 35 ♘c3 ♗xc3 35 ♗xc3 ♖xe4.

White's collapse deepened with **35 ♘f2? fxe4 36 ♘xe4 ♗xd5 37 ♛d3 ♛xb5**.

And it was completed when he passed up 38 ♛c2 or 38 ♛xb5 in favor of **38 ♘f6+? ♗xf6 39 ♖xg6+ hxg6 40 ♛xg6+ ♗g7 41 ♘g5**.

The threat was 42 ♛h7+ ♔f8 43 ♛f5+ with perpetual check but **White resigned** before 41...♛xb2 or 41...♛d7.

Swimming goes hand in hand with time pressure. A player who spent most of his allotted minutes gaining a winning advantage may feel that the bulk of his work is over. He can coast to the endgame or to the end of the time control.

110

The problem, as the previous game shows, is that converting an advantage, even a big one, often requires calculation late in the game.

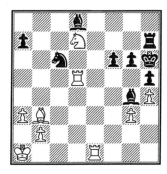

Kulaots – Alekseev
Moscow 2004

White to play

White has an extra Exchange and would like to trade pieces. He can try 32 ♘f8 ♖h8 33 ♘e6 but it gets messy after 33...♗a5 34 ♖e3 ♖e8.

The right way to exploit Black's poor piece coordination was 32 ♘b8!.

For example, 32...♘xb8 33 ♖xd8 ♘c6? 34 ♖d6 wins another pawn and 33...♘d7 34 ♗c2 followed by ♖g8 is also good for him.

Or 32...♗f3 33 ♘xc6 ♗xd5 34 ♘xd8, with an extra piece.

The main benefit of 32 ♘b8! is that he is eliminating Black pieces before they become active.

White was still much better after **32 ♘c5? ♗c7** but Black had a fixed target at g3, e.g. 33 ♖e3? ♘e7! and ...♘f5.

Play went **33 ♖c1! ♘e7 34 ♖d3 ♗e5 35 ♘e4 ♘f5.**

White to play

One of the tell-tale signs of swimming is when tactics seem to be more available to the defender than to the player with advantage. That is happening now.

There are no longer promising tactics based on attacking unprotected black pieces or the f6-pawn. Chances would be balancing after 36 ♖c6 ♗e2

37 ♖d2 ♗f3!. Moreover, the opportunities for favorable trades are disappearing, e.g. 36 ♗e6 ♖b7 37 ♖c2? ♘d4! and Black has the edge.

Variations like that should have been a warning to White and suggest safeguarding b2 with 36 ♔a2.

But he played **36 ♗d1?** and after **36...♖b7!** he needed to start thinking about how to draw.

He might have saved a half point with 37 ♖c5, or 37 ♖b1 ♗xd1 38 ♖dxd1 ♘xg3 39 ♘d6. Or even 37 ♖cc3 ♗xc3 38 bxc3.

But the rest was **37 ♖c2? ♗xd1 38 ♖xd1 ♘e3 39 ♖dd2 ♘xc2+ 40 ♖xc2 ♖b3 41 ♔a2 ♖e3 42 resigns**.

(6) The swindlee doesn't know when to panic.

It may seem that swindles always happen when a player overlooks tactics. But that is only a part of the story. Another part is misjudgment.

The swindlee believes he is winning easily when he is not. If he recognizes the truth in time, he can take corrective action: He can panic.

R. Byrne – C. Dominguez
Mar del Plata 1961

1 d4 ♘c6 2 ♘f3 d6 3 e4 ♗g4 4 ♗b5 a6 5 ♗a4 ♘f6 6 c4 ♘d7 7 ♗e3 e5 8 d5 ♗xf3 9 ♕xf3 ♘e7 10 ♘c3 ♘g6 11 h4! ♗e7 (11...♘xh4? 12 ♗xd7+ ♔xd7 13 ♕g4+) **12 h5 ♘f8 13 ♕g4! ♗f6 14 b4 h6 15 c5!**

White has a positional advantage on both wings. But his edge is greater on the queenside, where he can open the position favorably with c5-c6.

15...♗g5 16 0-0 ♘h7 17 ♗xg5 hxg5 18 c6 bxc6 19 ♗xc6 ♖b8 20 b5 axb5 21 ♘xb5

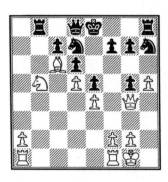

Black to play

So far this seemed like a textbook example of excellent positional play. White's simplest winning plan is to push his a-pawn to the seventh rank. An alternative is ♖fc1 followed by captures on d7 and c7.

But a good swindler knows when to change a losing positional battle to a tactical one. Black did it with **21...♞hf6! 22 ♛xg5 ♜xh5.**

His idea is ...♔e7! followed by ...♛h8!. For example, 23 ♛e3 ♔e7 24 f3! ♛h8. White will be on the defensive after, say, 25 ♝xd7 ♞xd7 26 a4 ♞c5.

The queenside seemed irrelevant after **23 ♛xg7 ♔e7!** in view of 24...♜h7 25 ♛g5 ♛h8!.

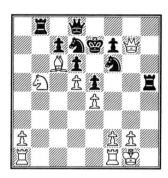

White to play

It was time to panic. If White looks for desperate measures he might find 24 ♝xd7 ♜h7 25 ♛xh7!.

He would be worse after 25...♞xh7 26 ♝f5 ♜xb5 27 a4. But he wouldn't be getting mated.

And he might have an impregnable fortress after 27...♜a5 28 ♝xh7 ♛a8 29 ♜fc1 ♔d8 30 ♜c4, for example.

He may even come out ahead if Black overplays his hand, with 24...♛xd7 (instead of 24...♜h7). Then he has 25 ♞a7! ♜bh8 26 ♞c6+ ♛xc6 27 ♛xh8! and 26...♔e8? 27 f3!.

But White couldn't accept the drastic turn of events. He chose **24 ♞a7??** and after **24...♜h7!** he was lost, **25 ♛g5 ♛h8!** in view of 26 f3 ♜b2 and ...♜h1 mate. Or 26 g3 ♜h1+ 27 ♔g2 ♛h3+ 28 ♔f3 ♜xf1.

White could also have lost a piece-down endgame after 25 ♝xd7 ♜xg7 26 ♞c6+ ♔xd7.

White didn't appreciate when his trouble began. It was 16 0-0? that gave Black his kingside chance.

If he had proceeded with the same queenside plan, 16 c6! bxc6 17 ♝xc6 ♜b8 18 b5, he would have had a big edge (18...axb5 19 ♞xb5 ♞h7 20 ♝xg5 and 21 a4) because there is no castled king to attack.

That misjudgment cost White the advantage. But he lost because he kept thinking about the queenside when it was time for desperate measures.

Misevaluations like that may be accidental. But there is also a skill to getting your opponent to misjudge a position and we'll examine it in the next chapter.

113

Quiz

13.

Giri – Svidler
Shenzen 2017

Black to play

White has just played 34 ♖f1 with a tactical idea 35 h3. That traps the h5-knight after 35...♕e6 36 g4! or 35...♕h4 36 ♘f5 ♕d8 37 g4.

Black played **34...g5~** and White replied **35 h3**. What did he overlook?

14.

Levitina – Marinello
Bloomington 1994

White to play

White won after **34 ♗xh6 ♔f7 35 e4**. What did the players miss?

15.

P. Smirnov – A. Smirnov
Samara 2014

Black to play

Black thought the pinning **37...♗f5** was a natural way to make progress. He won the endgame after **38 ♕f3 a5 39 ♕f4 a4** and **40 ♖e3 ♖xe4**.

What did both players miss?

16.

Nielsen – Sokolov
Reykjavik 2001

White to play

White can make slow but steady progress with 42 ♔c1 and 43 ♔b2. Once his king is secure he can advance the a- and b-pawns with the support of ♔a3.

But after **42 b4? h5 43 ♔c1?** he had given Black an opportunity. Which?

17.

Ivanchuk – Shirov
Dortmund 1992

White to play

White played **29 ♖e5** and explained that he was "blinded by his impending victory."

Why is this wrong and what should he have done?

Chapter Six:
False Narrative and Bluffing

We've seen several examples so far of players being victimized when they moved quickly. But even great players have been swindled when they had plenty of time to think rationally. Why?

One of the reasons is a false narrative: A player is surprised by his opponent's last move. He searches for an explanation and finds a logical one. But his idea of what is happening on the board is grossly wrong.

Taimanov – Fischer
Vancouver 1971

Black to play

This was played in the era when tournament games could be adjourned after the first forty moves.

White, and his two grandmaster seconds, foresaw this favorable position before play resumed. The three players, among the world's best, concluded Black would move his attacked queen to e5.

When he played **44...♛e4** instead, White was puzzled. Didn't that move allow 45 ♕c7+ and 46 ♖xf6 ?

He searched for an explanation until he found one: Bobby Fischer almost always preferred active defensive moves to passive play, he told himself. His queen is more aggressively placed on e4 than on e5. Fischer can create his own threat, of mate, with ...♖a2.

Convinced that he had figured out Bobby's thinking, he replied **45 ♕c7+**. Fischer answered with **45...♔h6**.

White to play

Now on 46 ♖xf6 Fischer will reply 46...♖a2, White thought. This must be why he played 35...♔h6. If he had tried 45...♔g8 then 40 ♖xf6 ♖a2?? would allow 41 ♕d8+ and ♕f8 mate.

With the king at h6 White has another resource. After 46 ♖xf6 ♖a2, he can force a trade of queens, 47 ♕f4+ ♕xf4 48 ♖xf4.

Black will reply 48...♖c2!, the best square for the defender's rook in such endgames. That active defense will probably be a draw. But at least I will be a pawn ahead, White thought.

It all made sense. So he played **46 ♖xf6??** and was stunned by **46...♕d4+**. White's king and rook are forked and after **47 ♖f2 ♖a1+** he had to lose the rook. He **resigned**.

What's the Point?

That blunder was not the result of a deeply set trap. Black didn't think, "I'll create a false impression with 44...♕e4." As Bobby Fischer famously said, "I don't believe in psychology. I believe in good moves."

No, on his own, White accidentally created a story about 44...♕e4. It was another case of one-player luck.

This is one of the pitfalls that becomes *more* likely as a player improves. When he is a beginner he doesn't look for an explanation of his opponent's last move. He chooses his own move without regard to it. Only when he is more experienced does he realize how important it is to figure out the reasoning behind his opponent's last move. What does it threaten? What is he planning?

The trouble, as Mark Taimanov found against Fischer, is that there may be more than one reason.

Portisch – Gligoric
Siegen 1970

Black to play

Quite lost, Black played **36...♕h3**. White easily understood the reason. It threatened to equalize material with 37...♕xh4.

White had a huge choice. Should he calculate the consequences of sharp moves such as 37 ♕xb7, 37 ♕xd6 or 37 ♖e8 ?

Or he should he protect the h4-pawn with 37 ♕e4 ? That prepares two good plans, 38 ♗c2 with a threat of ♕xh7 mate, or 38 ♗e6 ♕-moves 39 ♗f5 followed by ♗xh7.

In the end White chose what seemed like a more constructive move, **37 ♗c2**.

It prepares that mating plan, 37...b5?? 38 ♕e4!. It also sets a trap, 37...♕xh4?? 38 ♖h1. Then after the attacked queen moves away, ♖xh7 is mate.

And there was one more idea. White is poised to play a strong h4-h5-h6.

Black answered **37...♕g4.** White wondered why.

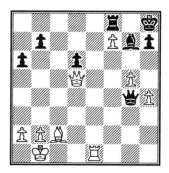

White to play

He easily spotted a reason. Black was discouraging 38 ♕e4 because 38...♕xe4 39 ♖xe4 ♖xf7 diminishes White's advantage.

White could have gone back to the ideas he was considering a move ago, 38 ♕xb7, 38 ♕xd6 or 38 ♖e8.

Each would have won, e.g. 38 ♕xb7 ♕xh4? 39 ♖h1! or 38 ♕xd6 ♕xh4? 39 ♖e8!.

But the fastest win seemed to be **38 h5**. Then 39 h6 is a deadly threat because the g7-bishop is attacked and 39...♗e5 40 ♖xe5! or 39...♗d4 40 ♕xd6 is lost.

However, there was another reason behind 37...♕g4. After 38 h5?? Black replied **38...♕b4!** and **White resigned** in view of 39...♕xb2 mate or 39...♕xe1+.

Birth of a False Narrative

That was another case of a self-inflicted wound, not a true swindle. But there are ways to craft a false narrative for your opponent to believe. This requires planting thoughts in his head.

Khalifman – Yuffa
Moscow 2006

Black to play

In a lost endgame, the little-known Black player chose **41...♖c7**. What's the point?

White was not just a grandmaster but a former FIDE world champion. He quickly deduced that Black intended 42...♖c3+ and 43...♖xh3.

Should White try to stop the check? No, 42 ♔d4? is met by 42...♖c4+. Also poor is 42 ♖d5 ♖c3+ 43 ♖d3 ♖c4.

White concluded that he couldn't protect his kingside pawns and also make progress towards a win. So he began calculating 42 ♖xb5 ♖c3+. He saw continuations such as 43 ♔d4 ♖xh3 44 ♖b8.

He knew from experience that this kind of position is usually a simple win. White advances the b-pawn with the support of his king. Black's king and kingside pawns are not a serious factor.

The problem is that ...♖c3+ was not the only idea behind 41...♖c7. The game went **42 ♖xb5?? ♖b7!**.

There were no winning chances in 43 ♖e5 ♖xb4 so the end was **43 ♖xb7 stalemate**.

Note how devious this was: After 41 ...♖c7 White could have won by bringing his king to the queenside, starting with 42 ♔d3 ♖f7 43 ♖xb5 ♖xf2 44 ♖e5 and 45 b5/46 ♔c4. or 43...♖f3+ 44 ♔d4 ♖xh3 45 ♖e5.

It seems more efficient to play 41...♖f7 so that Black can capture on f2 if the king runs to his left.

But **41...♖c7~** worked because it was more "understandable." If Black had played 41...♖f7, White would have said to himself, "Hmm, why doesn't 42 ♖xb5 win quickly?" Then he would have seen 42...♖b7! and the stalemate trap.

Waiting

A false narrative is often born in the mind of the swindlee while he is waiting for his opponent to move. The swindlee tries to guess what his opponent will do. When his guess turns out to be wrong – because another move is played – he begins to wonder what his opponent is thinking.

That is natural and proper. But it can lead to disastrous conclusions.

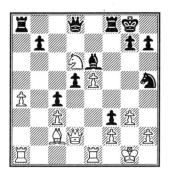

Cubas – Stupak
Baku 2016

Black to play

The position seems relatively even. But this is deceptive. Black has weak pawns at b7 and f3.

A computer-best continuation is 23...b6 24 ♖ab1 ♕c7 25 ♕e3 ♖ab8 26 ♗d1 with an evaluation of about +2.00.

Black sensed how bad his position was becoming and went desperate with **23...♘f4**. If allowed, he will play ...♕g5 and ...♘e2+ or ...♘h3+.

For example, 24 ♘xb7? ♕g5 (threat of 25...♘h3+ and ...♕xd2) 25 ♔h1 ♗h3 or 25 ♖e3 ♕g4 and Black wins.

After **24 gxf4 ♕h4** White understood that the immediate danger was 25...♕g4+ and 26...♕g2 mate.

There followed **25 ♔h1 ♖xf4**.

White to play

This is grossly unsound and can be refuted tactically, in a variation that begins with 26 &f5.

But White was now a piece up and felt he could win with simpler moves. He safeguarded his kingside with **26 &g1**.

He was winning after **26...&af8 27 &g3** because Black's ammunition was running low.

One of the remaining bullets – that is, tactical ideas – was 27...&h5 followed by ...&h4xh2+.

But White's extra piece would win after 28 &g1 &h4? 29 &g5!.

Another bullet was more disguised: After 27...&h3 Black would prepare ...&g2+.

That looks like just a check. But after, for example, 28 &xd5+ &h8 29 e6 Black wins with 29...&g2+ 30 &g1 &xh2+! 31 &xh2 &h4+ and mate.

But once again there is a defense. White can anticipate the check with 29 &g1 and then answer 29...&g2 with 30 &f5 or 30 &e6. That allows him to interpose a piece on h3.

For example, 30 &f5 &xh2+ 31 &xh2 &h4+ 32 &h3.

Black tried **27...&h8!?**.

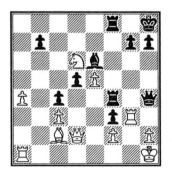

White to play

What's the point? Nothing is threatened.

If White searches for an explanation, he might conclude that Black is afraid of 28 ♖ag1.

That rook wasn't doing anything on a1. On g1 it would threaten 29 ♖xg7+ ♔h8 30 ♖xh7+, winning the queen. On g1 it seemed to provide extra protection against ...♗h3-g2+.

So, White chose **28 ♖ag1**. But the explanation he had for 27...♔h8 was a false narrative. Black's move was mainly a pass, a pass that also set a trap.

He mated with **28...♕xh2+!** and 29 ♔xh2 ♖h4+.

White didn't have anything to fear after 27...♔h8 and could have won with 28 ♕e3.

For example, 28...♕h5 still fails to 29 ♔g1 ♖h4 30 ♕g5 (or 29 ♗d1! ♖h4 30 ♗xf3).

The mating pattern that ended that game is familiar to experienced players. If they saw the position in a diagram, with the caption "Black to move and checkmate," many of them would find 28...♕xh2+ quickly.

But when the position occurred on his board White didn't recognize the pattern. He had been misled by 27...♔h8.

White falls victim to another common mating pattern in the next example. And again the best explanation of why it happens is a false narrative.

Gheorghiu – Liu Wenzhi
Lucern 1982

1 d4 ♘f6 2 c4 c5 3 d5 e6 4 ♘c3 exd5 5 cxd5 d6 6 ♘f3 g6 7 ♘d2 ♘bd7 8 e4 ♗g7 9 ♗e2 0-0 10 0-0 ♖e8 11 a4 ♘e5 12 ♖e1 a6 13 f4 ♘eg4 14 ♗f3 h5 15 ♘c4 ♘xe4 16 ♖xe4

White avoided 16 ♗xe4 ♕h4 and 16 ♘xe4 ♗d4+ 17 ♔h1? ♖xe4! and ...♘f2+. Another trap is 16 ♖xe4 ♗d4+ 17 ♔f1? ♘xh2+.

Next came **16...♗d4+ 17 ♖xd4 cxd4 18 ♘e4 ♕h4**.

White to play

White also dodged 19 h3 in view of 19...♗f5! 20 ♘cxd6 ♗xe4 with advantage.

For example, 21 ♗xe4 ♕f2+ 22 ♔h1 ♘f6 and 21 ♘xe4 f5 22 ♗xg4 ♖xe4 23 ♗e2 ♖ae8 or 22 hxg4 fxe4.

19 ♘cxd6! ♕xh2+ 20 ♔f1 ♗f5 21 ♘xf5 gxf5? 22 ♘f2!

White saw that if play continued 22...♘xf2 23 ♔xf2 Black would have one forcing move, 23...♕h4+.

Then 24 ♔g1?? ♖e1+ loses. But after 24 ♔f1 the worst that can happen is 24...♕h1+ 25 ♔f2 ♕h4+, with a perpetual check.

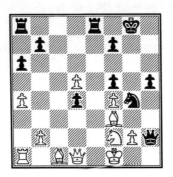

Black to play

While Black was thinking, White must have wondered if there is another reply to 22 ♘f2. He can find two.

One is 22...h4 with the idea of 23...♘xf2 24 ♔xf2 ♕g3+ 25 ♔f1 h3!, creating unclear complications.

But White can also see that 22...h4? is refuted by 23 ♗xg4! fxg4 24 ♕xg4+ with a killing counter attack. For example, 24...♔h8 25 ♖a3! and ♖h3. Or 24...♔f8 25 b3! and ♗a3+.

What else is there for Black in the diagram?

Well, there is 22...♖e3. It prepares 23...♖ae8 and ...♖e1+ and it is tactically justified by the fork 23 ♗xe3? ♘xe3+.

While Black thought, White must have wondered whether the best reply to 22...♖e3 was 23 ♖a3 or 23 ♗d2.

Nevertheless, when Black moved his choice was not 22...♘xf2, 22...h4 or 22...♖e3. It was **22...d3**.

124

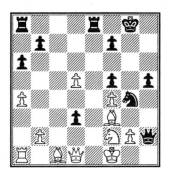

White to play

What's the point? The only obvious one was a transparent trap, 23 ♘xd3?? ♕h1 mate.

But if he looks further, White can see that 23...♖ac8! is a real danger. Black could follow with 24...♖c2! or 24...♖xc1! and ...♘e3+.

That looks ominous. But White can anticipate that with 23 ♖a3 and ♖xd3!, when he gets the advantage.

White had another idea. With **23 ♕xd3!** he would suddenly be close to winning. For example, 23...♖ac8 24 ♗xg4 followed by 25 d6, 25 ♗d2, 25 ♗e3 or just about anything.

Moreover, Black no longer has that perpetual check because 23...♘xf2 24 ♔xf2 ♕h4+ can be met by 25 g3! ♕h2+ 26 ♗g2.

Black replied **23...h4**.

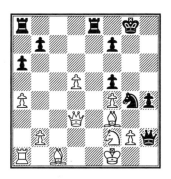

White to play

Now, I get it, White might say to himself. Black wanted to play 22...h4 on the previous move but, as I saw, that would allow 23 ♗xg4 fxg4 24 ♕xg4+.

By inserting 22...d3 and prompting 23 ♕xd3, Black is trying to improve that idea, e.g. 23 ♘xg4?? ♕h1+ 25 ♔f2 ♕e1 mate.

125

But Black has miscalculated **24 ♕xf5**, White thought. He intended 24...♘xf2 25 ♔xf2 ♕g3+ but that fails to 25 ♕g5+! and then 26 ♔xf2 wins for me.

Or so White thought. What he missed was **24...♕g1+!** and 25 ♔xg1 ♖e1 mate.

In retrospect, 22...d3? was a crude trap that gambled away a likely draw (22...♘xf2!) and a less forcing but also good 22...♖e3!.

As the game went, White should have won after 24 ♗d2, for example. But he believed a false narrative and paid the price.

"Could You Think Again"

Perhaps the most shocking trap in a modern world championship game came about from a false narrative. The winner said he didn't understand why his opponent could be so gullible.

Anand – Kasparov
World Championship, 11th game, New York 1995

1 e4 c5 2 ♘f3 d6 3 d4 cxd4 4 ♘xd4 ♘f6 5 ♘c3 g6 6 ♗e3 ♗g7 7 f3 0-0 8 ♕d2 ♘c6 9 ♗c4 ♗d7 10 0-0-0 ♘e5 11 ♗b3 ♖c8 12 h4 h5 13 ♔b1 ♘c4 14 ♗xc4 ♖xc4 15 ♘de2 b5 16 ♗h6 ♕a5 17 ♗xg7 ♔xg7 18 ♘f4 ♖fc8 19 ♘cd5 ♕xd2 20 ♖xd2 ♘xd5 21 ♘xd5 ♔f8 22 ♖e1 ♖b8 23 b3 ♖c5 24 ♘f4 ♖bc8 25 ♔b2 a5 26 a3

Black to play

Chances are roughly equal because White's knight is as good as Black's bishop and Black has lasting pressure on c2. Nothing much has changed in the last five moves. What should Black do?

He can seek a trade with 26...e5 27 ♘d5 ♗e6 and ...♗xd5. Also equal is 27 ♘d3 ♖5c7.

Or he can keep the knight off d5 with 26...e6 and 27...♔e7. This is tactically justified by 27 ♖xd6? ♖xc2+.

Or Black can pass, such as with 26...♔e8. Then on 27 ♘d5 he can reply 27...♗e6 and perhaps 28...♗xd5 29 exd5 ♔d7.

He played **26...♔g7** with what spectators said was a look of disappointment.

His e7-pawn is no longer protected,

27 ♘d5

Black to play

Spectators as well as grandmaster analysts expected 27...♔f8. That might be a tacit offer to repeat the position (28 ♘f4 ♔g7).

But 27...♔f8 could be risky in view of 28 ♘b6 and then 28...♖8c7 29 ♘xd7+ ♖xd7.

The double rook endgame favors White slightly after 30 e5 and exd6. For example, 30...d5 31 e6.

If White is more ambitious he could answer 27...♔f8 with 28 b4! axb4 29 axb4. Then 29...♖5c6 30 ♖a1! leaves Black's pieces somewhat passive.

And there's also a trap. Black would lose material after 29...♖c4 30 ♘b6! ♖xb4+ 31 ♔a3!.

But Black replied **27...♗e6** quickly. The spectators, on the 107th floor of the World Trade Center, began to buzz. What happens after 28 ♘xe7 ?

The answer seemed to be that 28...♖e8 29 ♘d5 ♗xd5 30 exd5?? ♖xe1 or 30 ♖xd5?? ♖xd5 would cost a rook.

But the outcome is not at all clear after the zwischenzug 30 b4! (30...axb4 31 axb4 ♖c4 32 ♖xd5 ♖xb4+ 33 ♔c3 ♖c4+ 34 ♔b3).

In any case, White went for a simpler line that seemed to promise a much bigger edge. He played **28 b4 axb4 29 axb4 ♖c4.**

White to play

This looks a lot like the position that could have arisen after 27...♔f8 28 b4!. The big difference is that Black's bishop is on e6, not under attack on d7.

Is that significant? White analyzed 30 ♘b6 ♖xb4+ 31 ♔a3 and could see that both rooks are attacked.

Black can limit his loss to an Exchange for a pawn with 30...♖4c4. But he would be worse after, for example, 31 ♘xc4 ♗xc4 32 ♔b4 ♖a8 33 e5. Or 31...♖xc4 32 ♖a1 and ♔b2.

So he played **30 ♘b6??** and after **30...♖xb4+ 31 ♔a3** ...

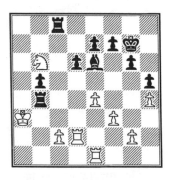

Black to play

...he was stunned by **31...♖xc2!**. He **resigned** in view of 32 ♔xb4 ♖xd2 and 32 ♖xc2 ♖b3+ 33 ♔a2 ♖e3+ and ...♖xe1.

So what happened here? In the worldwide post-mortems, it became evident that White had miscalculated beginning with 28 b4. He could have minimized the danger with 30 c3 and then 30...♗xd5 31 ♖xd5! ♖xc3 32 ♖e2, with drawing chances a pawn down.

Annotators suspected that 26...♔g7 – in connection with his facial expression – was a trap designed to convince White that he would be making progress with 27 ♘d5. When he quickly played 27...♗e6, he was indicating he had overlooked the continuation leading to 30 ♘b6.

After the game Garry Kasparov seemed almost insulted that his opponent believed this false narrative. "I mean, could you give another explanation than a complete lack of respect for him to think I didn't see it," he said. "Before playing ♘b6 he spent less than one minute. Before playing ♘b6 could you think again?"

Bluffing

Let's face it. Chessplayers bluff. When desperate, they make bizarre moves that have little rational basis for success. Unscrupulous opponents will bang down a move in your time trouble in the wild hopes of provoking a blunder.

More sophisticated bluffing is done with an appearance of calm confidence. The would-be swindler plays his moves as if he knows more about the position than you do.

Riazantsev – I. Sokolov
Poikovsky 2010

White to play

White is in trouble, perhaps lost, because of the powerful passed c4-pawn.

For example, 28 ♕a4 ♘fd5 29 ♖a1 c3. Black wins after 30 ♕xa5? ♕xa5 31 ♖xa5 c2.

Or 28 ♕e2 ♘fd5 29 ♖c1 c3 with ...c2 and ...♘c3/...♘a2 in mind.

White played **28 ♖c5** as if it were a strong move that Black had simply overlooked.

Black said it "put me in shock." He had ample time – about ten minutes to play 13 moves – to calculate the consequences.

He saw 28...♖xc5 29 dxc5 ♘xc2 would lose to 30 cxb6. Then the b-pawn is too strong (30...♘b4 31 ♘e5 and 32 b7).

He also saw 28...♘xc2 29 ♖xc8+ and realized 29...♔h7 30 ♘g5+ ♔h6 31 ♘xf7+ ♔h6 32 ♖h8+ would be a mate.

"For about two minutes I sat and wondered how I could not have noticed this resource," Black said.

In fact, 28 ♖c5?? was a blunder. Black could have decided the game with 28...♕xc5! (and 29 dxc5 ♘xc2 30 b6 ♘b4).

But after another minute of studying the position, Black chose **28...♖xc5??** and there followed **29 dxc5 ♕xc5**.

It wasn't clear, even after **30 ♕a4!**, that White's crisis was over. He could even have won immediately after 30...♕c7?? 31 ♖xb4! axb4 32 ♕a8+ ♔h7 33 ♘g5+ ♔h6 and now 34 b6! ♕xb6 35 ♘xf7+ and mates. Or 34...♕d7 35 b7.

Black could have drawn with 30...c3 31 ♕xa5 c2. But as often happened, the player who falls for a trap panicked **30...♘d3?? 31 ♕xa5 ♕xf2+ 32 ♔h2 ♘e4?? 33 ♕a8+ resigns**.

Believe Me

A bluff is a confidence game. The bluffer asks his victim to give him his trust.

Kiriakov – Voitsekhovsky
Nizhny Novgorod 1998

1 d4 ♘f6 2 c4 g6 3 ♘c3 ♗g7 4 e4 d6 5 ♘f3 0-0 6 ♗e2 ♘bd7 7 0-0 e5 8 ♗e3 ♖e8 9 d5 ♘g4 10 ♗g5 f6 11 ♗d2 f5 12 ♘g5 ♘f8 13 exf5 gxf5 14 ♗xg4! fxg4 15 f3 h6 16 ♘ge4 ♕h4 17 fxg4 ♗xg4 18 ♕b3 b6 19 ♖ae1 ♘h7 20 ♘b5 ♖ec8 21 ♕e3 a6 22 ♘bc3 ♖f8 23 b4 ♗f5 24 c5 bxc5 25 bxc5 dxc5 26 ♕xc5 ♘g5 27 ♗xg5 hxg5 28 ♕c6 ♔h8 29 ♖e3 ♗h7 30 ♖ef3 g4 31 ♖f7 ♗h6 32 g3 ♗e3+ 33 ♔h1

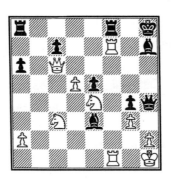

Black to play

Black could try 33...♕h6. It looks like a mistake because 34 ♖1f6 attacked the overloaded black queen (34...♕h5?? 35 ♖xf8+).

This means that 34...♖xf7 35 ♕xa8+ ♔g7 would follow.

But there is a trap – 36 ♖xh6?? ♖f1+ 37 ♔g2 ♖g1 is mate.

If White sees the trap he would play 36 ♖xf7+ ♔xf7 and have a sizable edge after 37 ♕d8 or 37 ♕c8.

The problem for Black is that he is lost whatever he does. There is no better move than 33...♕h6.

In mutual time trouble, Black gambled with **33...♕e7??!**. It is based on the same trap, 34 ♖xe7 ♖f1+ 35 ♔g2 ♖g1 mate.

"Everyone around our table saw the elementary 34 ♕xa8 and wins," Black recalled. "My opponent saw it."

Yet he didn't play it. This was one of those swindler's gambles that, from time to time, pays off.

White looked at 34 ♕xa8 and became convinced that 34...♕xf7 was a good reply. Why else would Black have played 33...♕e7 instead of 33...♕h6 ?

White's advantage would be slim after (34 ♕xa8 ♕xf7) 35 ♖xf7 ♖xa8 36 ♖xc7 ♖f8 because of Black's active pieces.

It didn't occur to him that there would be a ludicrously easy win (35 ♕xf8+!) instead.

White played **34 ♔g2??** because he "believed" his opponent. They drew after **34...♖xf7 35 ♕xa8+ ♔g7 36 ♕xa6?** (36 ♕c8!) **♗d4**.

Bluffs Called

A swindler doesn't always know when the tactical idea he is relying on is a bluff. To him it may look like the best try in a resignable position.

Here's another miraculous outcome and the result had nothing to do with a shortage of time.

Bouaziz – Miles
Riga 1979

Black to play

White has enough material to win in the long run. But he has two ways to win in the short run. He can push his c-pawn or he can double rooks on the eighth rank.

For instance, 39...♖a3 is computer-best. Then the first plan of 40 c5 and 41 c6 is convincing. White doesn't need an extra pawn (♖xh5).

Also lost is 39...♖c3 40 c5. But faster is 40 ♖e2, switching to the second winning plan of ♖d8 and ♖ee8.

Computers say Black's position now goes from bad to lost as he pursues an extravagant idea: getting his rook to h1 so he can play ...♖xh3. This would threaten ...♕h1 mate. White's king would take the rook on h1 and Black would respond with a series of queen checks.

White called Black's bluff, **39...♖e1? 40 c5! ♖h1 41 c6!**.

Black to play

He was right. His king is safe after 41...♖xh3 42 ♔xh3 ♕h1+ 43 ♔g3 and wins. Moreover, White has reached the 40-move time control and has plenty of time to consider what happens next.

When your bluff is called you may have no recourse but to make more moves that seem frightening. Computers like 41...♕b1 so that 42 c7 ♖g1+! and 43 ♕xg1 ♕xc2+ picks off the c7-pawn.

But the king would escape once more after 43 ♔h2! ♖h1+ 44 ♔g3!.

Therefore Black's **41...h4~** took away the escape square at g3. You can call that a bluff or you can see it as simply a better try than the losing 41...♕b1.

In either case, White could have won by pushing his pawn, 42 c7!. There is no mate – but it is hard to visualize 42...♖xh3 43 ♔xh3 ♕h1+ 44 ♕h2 ♕xf3+ 45 ♔xh4.

Only after the game was it obvious that White is winning, 45...♕xd5 46 c8(♕) or 45...♗e7+ 46 g5 ♕e4+ 47 ♔g3!.

White played it safe with **42 ♖cd2**. In this way he only had to calculate two forcing moves ahead (42...♖xh3? 43 ♖d1! ♖g3+ 44 ♕xg3!) rather than five or six. This was played in the days of adjournments so both players had ample time to consider the position overnight.

Black to play

Black tried to sow a bit of confusion with **42...♖c1!**, threatening 43...♖xc6.

White could have tried to win on the eighth rank with 43 ♖d8. This would have won quickly, e.g. 43...♖xc6 44 ♕xh4 with a threat of 45 ♖xf8+ ♔xf8 46 ♖d8 mate.

But **43 ♖c2** was good enough. Then 43...♖h1 would repeat the position that occurred after 41...h4. However, since the game was adjourned, White would have noticed 44 c7!, the move that he overlooked at move 42.

Black found a way to revive his tactical idea without repeating the position – **43...♕b1! 44 ♖dd2! ♖h1!**.

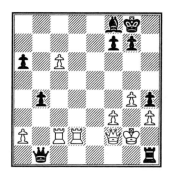

White to play

This time it wasn't a bluff: **45 c7 ♖xh3!** and **46 ♔xh3 ♕h1+ 47 ♕h2 ♕xf3+ 48 ♔xh4 ♗e7+ 49 g5 ♗xg5+!**. White **resigned** in view of and 50 ♔xg5 f6+ 51 ♔h4 g5 mate or 51 ♔g6 ♕g4 mate.

After the game it became clear that he would have won if he could have stopped that key ...♗e7+ move.

That means 45 g5 or 45 ♖e2 would have foiled 45...♖xh3.

In addition, it was found that the final error was not 45 c7?? but rather 46 ♔xh3??.

White could have saved a half point with 47 ♕f1!. Black can win the queen with 47...♖g3+ 48 ♔f2 ♖xf3+! 49 ♔xf3 ♕xf1+. But after 50 ♔e4! he should force perpetual check.

As usual, the swindlee wins the post-mortem. The swindler wins the game.

Quiz

18.

Volkov – Tkachiev
Moscow 2002

Black to play

Black can't stop the winning plan of a6-a7-a8(♕). He played **39...♕f6**.

What's the point? It seemed to be 40 a7 ♖xf3 41 ♖xf3?? ♕xa1+ and 41 a8(♕) ♖xf1+

Why avoided that with **40 ♗e4**. Is there anything wrong with that?

19.

Beliavsky – van der Wiel
Moscow 1982

White to play

(a) Evaluate the queen moves 23 ♕e2 and 23 ♕b3.

The game went **23 ♕e2 ♘d3+ 24 ♔d2 e4 25 ♗h4+ ♔f7 26 ♖hf1+ ♔g8 27 ♖xf8+ ♔xf8 28 ♖f1+ ♔g8 29 ♕h5 h6 30 b3 ♕d4 31 ♔e2 ♔h7**.

(b) Which White moves were errors?

20.

Tal – Kampenuss
Riga 1954

White to play

Tal was lost for most of the previous 20 moves. He chose **50 ♘h4**.

(a) What did Tal have in mind if Black had played 50...♕xh4 ?

(b) Did he have a better move?

Chapter Seven:
Panic Worthy

The experienced swindler takes desperate action when his position is objectively lost, or close to it. But what if it is merely bad?

Choosing the proper defense then is usually much harder than if the position is lost. The reason is that the defender may have a valid choice between the safe, passive move and the desperate, active one.

This choice often arises when material is equal but the defender has a significant positional disadvantage:

Averbakh – Spassky
Leningrad 1956

1 c4 ♘f6 2 ♘c3 g6 3 e4 d6 4 d4 ♗g7 5 ♗e2 0-0 6 ♗g5 c5 7 d5 ♕a5 8 ♗d2 a6 9 a4 e5? 10 g4! ♘e8 11 h4 f5 12 h5 f4 13 g5 ♕d8 14 ♗g4! ♘c7 15 ♗xc8 ♕xc8 16 ♘f3

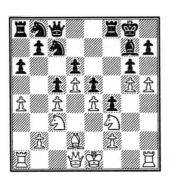

Black to play

It is easy to imagine White playing a standard attacking plan along the h-file. The moves could be ♖h4, ♔e2, ♕h1-h2 and ♖h1 followed by hxg6.

That is not the only powerful plan at White's disposal. Computers recommend passive play for Black, such as 16...♕d8 and ...♘d7, with a disadvantage of nearly 2.00.

Black decided to go desperate, **16...♘c6~**. It has been called "the most fantastic move played." But it is also a move that some fellow grandmasters would never play because it seems so "coffeehouse," so obviously an attempt to build a swindle.

After **17 dxc6 bxc6** White had a winning material advantage. Computers say his advantage had grown to +3.00.

But Black can now improve his side of the board, with ...♘e6-d4, for instance.

White to play

White came close to winning after **18 ♘h4 ♛e8 19 hxg6 hxg6 20 ♛g4 ♖b8 21 ♘d1 ♘e6 22 ♖a3! ♘d4 23 ♖ah3 ♛f7 24 ♗c3 ♖fe8 25 ♖3h2 ♛xc4 26 ♘xg6.**

But Black rebounded after **26...♖e6 27 ♗xd4? ♖xg6 28 ♛f5 ♛e6 29 ♛xe6+ ♖xe6 30 ♗c3 d5 31 f3 ♖b3 32 ♖h3 c4 33 ♔d2 ♖g6 34 ♖g1 d4** thanks to his c- and d-pawns.

A turning point came after **35 ♗a5 ♗f8 36 ♖g4 ♖d6 37 ♔c2 ♖d7 38 g6 ♖db7 39 ♗e1 c5 40 ♖gh4 ♗g7** with **41 ♗a5? c3! 42 bxc3 ♖a3!.**

Black was the one pressing for a win after that and *he* was the unlucky one when the game was drawn, after **43 cxd4 exd4 44 ♖xf4 ♖a2+ 45 ♔d3 ♖b1 46 ♖h1 ♖xa4 47 ♔c2 ♖b5 48 e5 d3+ 49 ♔xd3 ♖xf4** and so on.

Hang Tough

The alternative to desperation is typically hang-tough, passive defense. Paul Keres was a master of hanging tough. But he had a superb sense of when passive was inferior to active. He knew when to try to confuse an opponent.

Boey – Keres
Varna 1962

1 e4 ♘c6 2 d4 e5 3 dxe5 ♘xe5 4 f4 ♘g6 5 ♘f3 ♗c5 6 ♗c4 d6 7 ♛e2 ♘f6? 8 f5! ♘e7 (**8...♘e5 9 ♘xe5 dxe5 10 ♗xf7+! ♔xf7 11 ♛c4+) 9 ♘c3 0-0 10 ♗g5! c6 11 0-0-0 ♛c7? 12 ♖hf1**

137

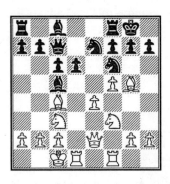

Black to play

Keres has played the opening so badly he might have lost a miniature after 12 e5!. For example, 12...dxe5 13 ♗xf6 gxf6 14 ♘e4. Or 12...♘fd5 13 ♗xd5 ♘xd5 14 ♖xd5! cxd5 15 ♘xd5 with a powerful attack.

But 12 ♖hf1 has its points. It prepares a powerful rook lift, ♖f3-h3, after ♗xf6/...gxf6. Also, a delayed 13 e5! dxe5 14 ♘xe5 may be stronger with the f5-pawn protected.

Some computers endorse the hang-tough defense, 12...♘e8. But good defenders – not to mention good swindlers – distrust a retreat like that.

If you give computers a nudge they tend to confirm that 13 e5 dxe5 14 ♘xe5 would be a strong answer (14...♘d6 15 f6!).

So would 13...d5 14 f6 and 13...♘xf5 14 ♘e4 or 14 g4.

Keres chose **12...b5~** and **13 ♗b3 a5!**.

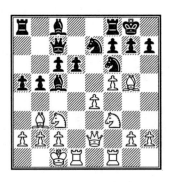

White to play

The threat of 14...a4 gave White something to worry about. That is what a swindler wants. He wants White to start defending, with 14 a3 b4 or 14 a4 b4 15 ♘b1 d5.

White would have to calculate 14 e5! to realize it is the best move. The complications are great after 14...dxe5 and then 15 ♗xf6 gxf6 16 ♘e4.

Put yourself in White's chair:

Could you analyze 16...a4 17 ♘xf6+ ♔g7 in your head and see that 18 ♘h5+? ♔h8 is bad for you?

And would you see 18 ♘e8+! ♖xe8 19 f6+! so that 19...♔g8 20 ♗xf7+! ♔xf7 21 ♘xe5+ ?

You might also consider 15 ♘xe5, rather than 15 ♗xf6. Then 15...a4 16 ♗xf7+ is crucial. It takes some skill to see that 16...♖xf7 17 ♘xf7 ♔xf7 18 ♗xf6 and 19 ♘e4! is a big White edge.

And it is not easy to see that 15...♘xf5, instead of 15...a4, favors White solidly after 16 ♗xf6 gxf6 17 ♘g4! – but 17 ♕g4+ ♘g7 does not.

In the end, White got confused. He opted for a plan consistent with his last move, **14 ♗xf6? gxf6 15 ♘d4.**

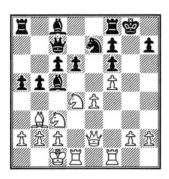

Black to play

He had cleared the way for 16 ♕g4+ ♔h8 17 ♕h4. That would threaten ♕xf6+ and prepare ♖f3-h3.

Computers spend time on 15...♕a7 or 15...♕b6. Then 16 ♕g4+ ♔h8 17 ♕h4 is refuted by 17...♗xd4, guarding f6.

But when the swindler feels the tide shifting in his direction, he goes for blood. Keres played **15...a4!**.

Now White could see 16 ♕g4+ ♔h8 17 ♕h4 is met by 17...♘g8.

There are immense complications after 18 ♖f3 axb3 19 ♖g3, threatening 20 ♕g4 and mate. Then 19...d5 allows the defense 20 ♕g4 ♕xg3 and 21...bxa2.

In any case, the bewildered White chose **16 ♖f3? axb3.**

But there was no mating attack (17 ♖g3+ ♔h8 18 ♕g4 ♖g8). He **resigned** soon after **17 ♘xc6 ♕xc6.**

How Lost?

Good swindlers have a sophisticated sense of when to panic. The factors that go into that decision include:

(a) *How lost am I? How difficult will it be for my opponent to convert his advantage?* If all he needs are routine moves to carry out a crushing plan, then the moment is panic-worthy. But if he still needs to find some difficult moves, desperation may be premature.

(b) *How trappy is the position?* Are there possibilities for tactical mistakes my opponent can fall into?

(c) *How much time does he have?* Swindles occur most often in tournament games when the victim has only a few minutes to make critical decisions.

The first question is not something many players want ask themselves. The answer might depress them.

But to the experienced swindler, the answer frees his mind. If it is "*I am quite lost*" then he can feel more confident about going desperate. If it is "*Maybe not totally lost*" then he should consider a hang-tough defense.

What decision would you make in the next diagram?

Czerniak – Graf-Stevenson
Mar del Plata 1942

1 e4 ♘c6 2 d4 d5 3 e5 ♗f5 4 g4 ♗d7 5 ♘h3 e6 6 c3 ♘ce7 7 ♗e3 c5? 8 dxc5! ♘c6 9 f4! ♘h6 10 ♗d3 ♕h4+ 11 ♘f2 0-0-0 12 ♘d2

Black to play

A pawn down, Black faces the prospect of a crushing queenside attack with 13 b4 and 14 b5. or White could play 13 ♘f3 and drive Black's pieces into passivity.

If Black tries to break the center open with 12...f6?? her queen is trapped by 13 ♘f3.

If she prepares for ...f6 with 12...♛e7, both 13 b4 and 13 ♘f3 promise a virtually winning advantage.

Black went for **12...d4~**. It is based on her best tactical resources, the possibility of opening the d-file and the c6-h1 diagonal.

For example, 13 cxd4 ♘xd4! 14 ♗xd4 ♗c6:

White to play

Black regains material because of her threats of 15...♗xh1 and 15...♖xd4. After 15 ♗e3? ♖xd3! Black has a substantial edge.

But that's a best-case scenario. White can obtain a powerful counterattack by giving back a piece with 15 ♘f3 ♗xf3 16 ♛xf3 ♖xd4.

Then he avoids the equalizing 17 ♖c1? ♘xg4! and plays 17 0-0.

The game could end soon after 17...♗xc5 18 ♖ac1.

Instead, White played the move that seemed to win without complications, **13 ♘f3!.**

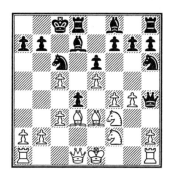

Black to play

Now 13...♛e7 14 cxd4 leaves Black gasping for air. That's not why she chose 12...d4.

Her idea was a desperation sacrifice, **13...dxe3~ 14 ♘xh4 exf2+ 15 ♔xf2 ♗xc5+.**

141

Was this better than hanging tough with 12...♕e7 ? Not according to computers, who say White's advantage is greater after 15 ♔xf2.

But humans will prefer to give up the queen for two pieces – and be active – than to be a mere pawn down with dreadful pieces and facing a crushing queenside attack.

At least here, White is the one with an insecure king and his center can be undermined, with ...g5.

There are credible scenarios in which Black would be back in the game, such as 16 ♔e1 g5 17 fxg5 ♘xe5! 18 gxh6? ♗c6!.

Naturally, there are improvements for White, such as 17 ♘f3! or 18 ♘f3. But traps are beginning to appear.

They began to multiply after **16 ♔g3 g5! 17 ♘f3! gxf4+ 18 ♔xf4 ♖hg8**.

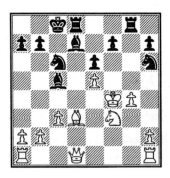

White to play

White should still win but Black is getting more tactics than she seemed to deserve. For example, 19 h3 f5! and 20 gxf5 ♘e7! is quite good for Black because of 21...♘d5+.

Instead, 20 exf6 is called for. But then comes 20...e5+!.

Black would win after 21 ♔e4?? ♘xg4!. He would not be worse after 21 ♘xe5? ♘xe5 21 ♔xe5 ♗e3! threatens mate with 22...♖ge8+. (But justice should prevail after 21 ♔g3!.)

After **19 g5** Black found **19...♘e7!**, again with a strong ...♘d5+ or ...♗c6 on tap (20 gxh6?? ♘d5+ 21 ♔e4 ♖g4 mate).

To stay on the road to victory White has a wide choice that includes 20 ♗e4 and 20 ♕b3.

But he preferred to stop ...♘d5+ with **20 c4**. The decisive point arose after **20...♗c6!**.

White to play

Now on 21 gxh6 Black has 21...f5!, threatening ...♖g4 mate.

Then 22 h3 is no defense because of 22...♖g2! and ...♘g6 mate (or 23 ♘h4 ♖d4+).

White's best would be 22 exf6! and the endgame edge of 22...♖xd3! 23 ♕xd3 ♘g6+ 24 ♕xg6 ♖xg6.

But White didn't realize that Black's last move contained another idea. After **21 ♕e2? ♖xd3! 22 ♕xd3 ♘g6+** he had to play **23 ♕xg6 fxg6!** and lost after ...♖f8+.

How Easy?

Compare that game with another desperation queen sacrifice.

Tolush – Geller
Moscow 1952

1 d4 ♘f6 2 c4 g6 3 ♘c3 ♗g7 4 e4 d6 5 f3 0-0 6 ♗e3 e5 7 ♘ge2 ♘bd7 8 ♕d2 ♘b6 9 b3 exd4 10 ♘xd4 ♖e8 11 ♗e2 c6 12 0-0 d5? 13 exd5 ♕e7 14 ♗f2 cxd5 15 c5

Black to play

In contrast with the last game, Black got out of the opening with equal material. But he would be in poor shape positionally after 15...♘bd7 16 b4 or 16 ♖ae1 ♕d8 17 ♘db5.

Computers called that a disadvantage of about +1.00. His pieces would be restricted but not nearly as much as Black's after 12 ♘d2 in the previous game.

Nevertheless, Black chose **15...♕xc5~**. He knew White, a strong grandmaster, would have a powerful discovered attack on his queen when he moved his d4-knight.

And he could see that 16 ♘f5 ♕b4 17 ♘xg7 ♔xg7 18 ♗d4 would be a very unpleasant position to defend and easily lost.

His idea was **16 ♘f5 ♕xf2+! 17 ♖xf2 ♗xf5**.

White to play

He obtained two minor pieccs and a pawn for the queen. That's about what Black got in the last game.

What helped him decide on the sacrifice were threats and traps. He is ready to play 18...d4! so that 19 ♕xd4? ♘fd5 and wins.

Or 19 ♘b5 ♘fd5 20 ♘xd4? ♖ad8 when there is trouble brewing on the d-file (21 ♖d1? ♘e3!).

There is another criterion in a swindler's desperation decision: How easy will it be for my opponent for find good moves?

White found a good one, **18 ♘b5!**, but after **18...♖ad8** the onus was still on him.

White to play

144

Black knew ...d4 would be a good move if he can play it. A plausible continuation would be 19 ♖ac1 d4 20 ♗d3 ♗xd3 21 ♕xd3 ♘fd5 followed by occupying e3, c3 or f4.

The game could quickly turn around after natural moves, 22 f4 a6 23 ♘c7 (or 23 ♘a3) ♖e3 24 ♕d2 ♘c3. It doesn't take a blunder by White or a brilliant one by Black.

As it turned out, the best White move was hard to find (19 ♘xa7) – and a bad one was easy, **19 ♘d4??**.

After **19...♘e4!** White had to give back material. Black would have enough compensation for the queen with 20. fxe4 dxe4 21. ♕a5 ♗xd4.

The chances were almost equal after **20 ♕b4! ♘xf2 21 ♔xf2** (20...♘c4!) and Black won after mutual errors.

Other Criteria

There are other questions the defender can ask when he decides whether to panic:

Are my chances of drawing with the safe move greater than my chances of losing with it? And do I have any realistic chances of *winning* with the risky move?

The answers to these questions are often subjective. They vary depending on how ambitious, optimistic or aggressive the defender is.

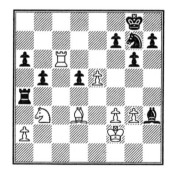

J. Polgar – Grischuk
Linares 2001

White to play

Computers say 37 ♘c1 would keep Black's advantage in the -2.00 range. That makes sense because he is two pawns ahead.

Is that enough to win? The answer is "Probably."

Another question White can ask herself is: How easy would winning be? Would it require finding difficult moves?

Here the answer is "Probably not." Routine moves, such as 37...h5 and later ...g5 should eventually do the job.

That suggests that White needs a dramatic change and she started with **37 g4~.** That threatens 38 ♖c8+ and also cuts off the bishop's escape from h3.

Black to play

Black would like to insert 37...♖xa2+ 38 ♔g3. Then 38...♘e6 would be forced, so that 39 ♔xh3 ♘f4+.

To play this, Black would have to calculate 39 ♖xe6 and 39...fxe6 40 ♔xh3, regaining some material.

But the pieces are no match for the queenside pawns after 40...♖a3 41 ♗c2 a5 or 40...b4.

Better is 39 ♘c5. Black's advantage diminishes after 39...♘xc5 40 ♖xc5 ♗g2? (40...♖d2!) 41 ♖xd5.

And Black didn't have enough time to check out 39...♖g2+! 40 ♔xh3 ♘f4+ 41 ♔h4 h6!, with a threat of 42...g5 mate.

The complications convinced Black to reject 37...♖xa2+!. He took the easy way out, **37...h5?.**

White forced his hand with **38 ♘c5!** and then **38...♖xa2+ 39 ♔g3 hxg4 40 fxg4.**

Black to play

All of a sudden White has serious counterplay, e.g. 40...♗g2 41 ♖c8+ ♔h7 42 ♘d7! and ♘f6+.

Black can stop that with 40...♘e6 or with the tactical 40...♖a3 41 ♔xh3 ♘e6.

The latter leads to a rook endgame, 42 ♘xe6 ♖xd3+ 43 ♔h4 fxe6 44 ♖xa6. Black can even lose (44...♖e3 45 ♔g5 ♖xe5+ 46 ♔xg6 ♔f8 47 ♔f6). The game would be drawn after 44...d4 45 ♔g5.

Black thought he had better chances with bishops on the board. But White had sufficient play after **40...♘e6 41 ♘xe6 fxe6 42 ♗xg6**.

A draw was agreed soon after **42...♔g7 43 ♗h5 ♗f1 44 ♖xe6 b4 45 ♖g6+ ♔h8**. White could easily have gotten the upper hand, 42...♗f1 43 ♖xe6 ♗c4 44 ♔f4 b4 45 ♔g5 b3 46 ♖b6 b2?? 47 ♔f6 and wins.

Bottom line: White should have lost faster after 36 g4~. But it was by far the best practical chance. There were even ways for White to gain the advantage.

No Clear Answer

A player skilled in hang-tough defense may disagree with White's choice in the last game. What about this game? Black is not clearly lost.

Norwood – Plaskett
Eastbourne 1990

Black to play

White threatens 26 ♗b7, trapping the queen (26...♕a3 27 ♖a1).

Black can give up the Exchange, 25...♖c7 26 ♗e5 ♕c8 27 ♗xc7 ♕xc7. But even with his extra pawn he would be significantly worse.

An experienced defender – not just a swindler – would try to distract White by offering a choice. After 25...e5 Black would be alive following 26 ♗xe5 ♕e6.

But if White makes the right decision, 26 ♗b7! ♕e6 27 ♗xc8 ♖xc8, he again has good winning chances. (Remember this position.)

After 28 ♕e2 a6 29 ♖a5, for example, it would be harder for Black to draw than for White to win.

Black felt his situation was dire and went for **25...♘d5~**. It was partially based on 26 cxd5?? ♕xb5 and 26 ♗xd5? exd5 27 ♖xd5 ♗e7 with near-equality.

He was mainly betting that he would find counterchances if White replied 26 ♖xc5! ♖xc5 27 cxd5.

Black to play

The key question that Black faced at move 25 was whether this position would be better than the one resulting from 25...e5 26 ♗b7.

Black can achieve rough material equality with 27...♕c4 28 ♖d3 exd5.

But those bishops are powerful if White turns to kingside attack, for example after 29 ♕c2 followed by ♗d4 and ♕g4.

Black couldn't be sure of that when he chose 25...♘d5. All he could hope was that he could exploit the pin on the c-file.

But he can't – 27...♖fc8 fails to 28 d6 ♖xc3? 29 d7.

If 28...♕a3, White would be winning after 29 ♖d3 ♖xc3 30 d7 or 29 d7 ♖d8 30 ♖d3.

But there was one other option for White and it occurred on the board: **26 ♖a1?** overlooked Black's threat, **26...♕xb5! 27 cxb5 ♘xc3** (28 ♕xc3?? ♗xf2+).

White to play

The position is slightly better for White. Black can anchor his bishop on d4 with ...e5. He may also be able to use tactics to liquidate the queenside pawns, bringing the position closer to a draw, e.g. 28 ♗c6 ♗d4 29 ♖a5 a6!? 30 ♖xa6 ♘xb5.

But the jarring effect of a swindle took effect and play went **28 ♖a6? ♗b6 29 ♕b3 ♘e2+ 30 ♔h2? ♗xf2 31 ♕f3? ♗xg3+ 32 ♔h1 ♖c1+** and Black eventually won.

So was Black's decision to choose 25...♘d5 over 25...e5 correct?

The experienced swindler would say "Yes" because White had three ways to go wrong (26 cxd5??, 26 ♗xd5? and 26 ♖a1?).

The experienced defender would say "No!" because 26 ♖xc5! would have given White better winning chances than after 25...e5.

Crazy Time

The last major factor in a swindler's decision to panic is the clock. In a tournament game, the amount of time the opponent has left is often crucial. Good players make crazy moves when they have minutes, if not seconds, left.

Hort – R. Weinstein
Leipzig 1960

White to play

It's not obvious yet but White's king is the one in grave peril. Black threatens to win quickly with 33...g4 (34 ♗e2 gxh3).

Black has a second winning idea, 33...♘xf3 so that 34 gxf3 ♗c8 and ...♗xh3. Or 34 ♖xf3 ♕xe4.

Computers look at 33 ♕d2 so that 33...g4? 34 ♕xf4 or 33...♘xf3 34 ♕d7+ saves White.

But engines eventually conclude that Black is close to winning after 33...♔g6 followed by 34...♕e6 and ...♘xf3, or the immediate 33...♕e6.

Add to this the mutual time pressure and this becomes prime panic time. White chose **33 ♖c1~** with the threat of ♖c7+ and ♖xb7.

149

Black to play

Of course, Black looked at both 33...g4 and 33...♘xf3 because White's last move didn't stop either of them.

For example, 33...g4 34 ♖c7+ ♔g6 35 ♖xb7 and now 35...gxf3 is good.

But 35...gxh3! threatens 36..hxg2 mate and wins after 36 gxh3 ♕c8!.

It also looks like the alternative in the diagram, 33...♘xf3, wins after 34 ♖c7+ ♔g6 35 ♖xb7 ♘xg1. But 34 ♖xf3 isn't so clear.

Besides, White's last move also handed Black a knight fork. Doesn't it win faster?

Once Black saw that his king would be relatively safe on g6, the game went **33...♘d3! 34 ♖c7+ ♔g6 35 ♕d4**.

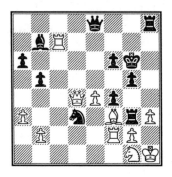

Black to play

White must have expected 35...♘xf2+ 36 ♕xf2. Then the threat of ♖xb7 seems to allow time for counterplay with 37 ♘e2 or even 37 e5.

That was a mirage. Black would win after 36...♗xe4!. Then 37 ♘e2 ♖xf3 or 37...♖hxh3+ 38 gxh3 ♖xh3+ would end resistance soon. Also lost is 37 ♕a7 ♗xf3 38 ♖g7+ ♔h6.

So was 30 ♖c1 just a bad move?

If all that mattered was the size of Black's advantage with 35...♘xf2+ 36 ♕xf2 ♗xe4 – compared to the one after 33 ♕d2 ♔g6 or 33...♕e6 – then White had definitely worsened his position. It had become "loster."

But 30 ♖c1 cost Black precious minutes to sort out the possibilities. He found **35...♕d8!**, which is at least as good as 35...♘xf2+. They key point is 36 ♕xd8 allows Black to win a full rook with 36...♘xf2+ and 37...♖xd8.

He must have expected White to resign soon after **36 ♖d7 ♘xf2+ 37 ♔h2 ♕c8!**.

White to play

Black's advantage has ballooned to more than -6.00, according to some computers. They recommend 38 ♖d6 ♕f8 39 ♖b6. But they acknowledge that 39...g4, among others, would win.

But there were still three moves to go before the time control. White's **38 ♕d6** was another surprise. It threatens ... to threaten.

If Black does nothing, White will play 39 ♕e7 or 39 ♕e6 and the mate threats would force the unclear 39...♕xd7 40 ♕xd7.

Black has several ways to win. But with seconds left it was hard to see, for example, that 38...♗xe4! 39 ♕e7 ♘g4+! is a forced mate. Or that 38...♖hxh3+! also wins quickly.

Fastest of all was 38...♕c1! followed by 39...♖hxh3+! and mate next.

But he was too worried about his own king to think of mating White. He chose **38...♗a8** and, for the first time in several moves, White replied with the objectively best move, **39 ♕e6!**.

Black to play

151

If he had more time Black might have replied 39...♛xd7 40 ♛xd7, ending White's mating threats and leaving an unclear outcome after 40...♝xe4.

But he chose **39...♛f8.** Computers like it. It also offers much greater winning chances.

The next move would be the last of the time control. White could have played 40 ♛f5+ quickly to avoid forfeiting. But there would be no follow-up after the forced 40...♚h6.

White needed to give his opponent one last choice and he did it with **40 ♘e2!**.

The g3-rook is trapped but the main threat is not 41 ♘xg3. It is 41 ♘xf4+! gxf4 42 ♛f5+ ♚h6 43 ♛h5 mate.

Black could have saved himself with 40...♖xf3! 41 gxf3 and then 41...♝c6. But the game ended with **40...♖h6?? 41 ♛f5 mate**.

Of course, 40...♖h6 was a blunder. But almost as bad was 38...♝a8??, which missed at least three forced wins and created an even position. Such mistakes are possible when a swindler takes risks with moves like 33 ♖c1~, 36 ♖d7~ and 38 ♛d6~.

Chapter Eight:
The Swindling Process

A successful swindle is most dramatic when it is brought about by a single surprise move.

**Vachier-Lagrave –
Wang Hao**
Wijk aan Zee 2011

Black to play

White is ready to mate. He can do it by moving his knight, followed by ♖h3 and ♕h8. Or he could do it with ♗e7 followed by ♘g5 and ♕h7.

Once again, computers are masochists. They suggest delaying sacrifices such as 31...♘c2 32 ♘g1 ♗c3 or the doomed defense 31...♘c6 32 ♘g1 f5 33 exf6.

Black's **31...♕b5~** left White with that choice of ways to win. That was a good thing for Black.

There would have been no defense to the first idea, retreating a knight with 32 ♘g1! or 32 ♘d2! followed by ♖h3.

But in a tactical position, an advance, **32 ♗e7**, seemed better. In addition to freeing g5 for his knight, White's move cut off the escape square at f8 and added pressure to the pinned b4-knight.

What he missed was **32...♘d3!!**. The rook on b3 is hanging and after **33 ♖xb5** Black replied **33...♘f4+**.

Then **34 ♔f1??** ♖c1+ is suicide. The game ended with **34 ♔g3 ♘e2+ 35 ♔h3 ♘f4+** and a draw by perpetual check.

White could have continued the game with 34 ♔h1 ♖c1+ 35 ♘g1. But after 35...♘e2 36 h3 ♖xg1+ 37 ♔h2 axb5 and ...♖b1xb2 chances are in balance.

There was a way for White to play to win, with 33 ♖xd3 (rather than 33 ♖xb5) and then 33...♕xd3? 34 ♘g5. But that allows 33...g5! so that 34 ♘xg5 ♕xd3 and the queen defends h7 and Black wins.

It Takes Two

Swindling is often more than a shock-move such as 32...♘d3. Often it is a two-step process. First, the swindlee makes an error that throws away his large advantage. But he is not losing – yet. That takes a second error.

Byrne – Korchnoi
Sousse 1967

1 e4 c5 2 ♘f3 d6 3 d4 cxd4 4 ♘xd4 ♘f6 5 ♘c3 ♘c6 6 ♗e3 g6 7 f3 ♗g7 8 ♕d2 0-0 9 ♗c4 ♕a5 10 0-0-0 ♗d7 11 ♔b1 ♖fc8 12 ♗b3 ♘e5 13 h4 ♘c4 14 ♗xc4 ♖xc4 15 ♘b3 ♕a6 16 e5! ♘e8 17 ♘d5 ♗xe5 18 ♘xe7+ ♔f8 19 ♘d5 ♗f5? 20 ♗h6+ ♘g7 21 ♘e3!

Now 21...♖a4 is poor after 22 ♘xf5 gxf5 23 f4 ♗f6 24 ♕xd6+. So is 21...♖c6 22 ♘xf5 gxf5 23 ♖he1 or 22 g4 ♗e6 23 f4 ♗f6 24 g5.

Viktor Korchnoi recognized what a doomed position was. He chose **21...♖ac8~**, so that 22 ♘xf5? ♖xc2!. Play went **22 ♘xc4 ♖xc4 23 ♖c1 ♖a4 24 f4** and Black was running out of ideas after **24...♗f6 25 ♗g5**.

Black to play

Computer-best is 25...♘e8 and 26 ♗xf6 ♘xf6. It leaves White a few problems to solve after 27 ♕c3 ♖xf4 (28 ♕xf6?? ♗xc2+).

But Black bet on **25...♗xg5~ 26 hxg5 ♖xa2**.

This is risky because after 27 ♖cd1 or 27 ♕c3 his survival chances are worse than in the 25...♘e8 line. For instance, 27 ♖cd1 ♖a4 28 ♖xh7 threatens a quick finish with 29 ♕c3!.

White's advantage would be prohibitive after 28...♖c4 29 ♖h8+ ♔e7 30 ♘d4 (30...♖a4 31 ♕e2+).

But White made his first error of the game, **27 ♖xh7??**.

Black quickly played his only good reply, **27...♗e6**.

White to play

White didn't appreciate how much had changed. Now he is the one who needs desperate measures.

After the game, 28 ♖h8+! ♔e7 29 c4 ♗f5+ 30 ♖c2 was found, so that 30...♕xc4 31 ♕e3+ ♘e6 32 ♔xa2 ♗xc2 33 ♔a3 ♕a6+ 34 ♔b4 might save the game.

But his first blunder was quickly followed by the second, **28 ♕c3?? ♖a1+!** and **White resigned** before 29 ♘xa1 ♕a2 mate.

That was a dramatic example because the two mistakes were gross errors. A game-losing error is usually easily identifiable. But a previous error may not be obvious.

de Firmian – Shirazi
Estes Park 1986

Black to play

The tactics are temporarily running in White's favor. They allow him to remain two pawns up, 26...♖xf2?? 27 ♕h4+. Or 26...♕a5 27 ♕xc6 ♕xa2? and 28 ♕xd6 ♕xb1 29 ♕xf8+.

Computers like 26...♕d7, which prepares ...♖e8. But unless something changes drastically and soon, the two extra pawns will decide the game. After 27 ♗e3 ♖e8 28 ♕f3 or 28 ♕g6, for example, White can consolidate further (♔g1 and ♖c1) before making progress with c3-c4.

155

Black chose **26...♕f7** because it attacks two pawns – but also makes his queen more active. After 27 ♗e3 ♕xa2 Black would have counterplay (...a5-a4) and real survival chances.

The drawback was **27 ♕xc6**.

Black to play

This looked dangerous in view of 27...♕xf2 and 28 ♕xd6? ♕e1+ 29 ♔h2 ♖f1. The threat of 30...♖h1 mate would be decisive.

But 27...♕xf2 could be safely answered by 28 ♗e3!. White is still on track after 28...♕xe3 29 ♕xd6 threatens ♕xf8+.

A win would become clearer after 29...♔g8 30 ♕d5+ ♔h8 31 ♕xb5 ♕xc3 32 ♕c5!, for instance.

The same goes for 28...♕xa2 29 ♕xb5. White would have solved most of his tactical problems.

Black chose **27...♕g6!**. This looks strange. Didn't Black put his queen on f7 so he can attack f2 and a2?

But now the tactics are beginning to help Black – 28 ♕xb5?? loses to 28...♖xf2.

White can avoid mate on g2 or f1 with 29 ♗g5. But then 29...a6 overloads the queen (30 ♕d5 ♕xb1+ or 30 ♕b6 ♕xg5 31 ♕xd6 ♕xg2 mate).

Instead, White tried **28 ♖xb5**. The drastic change Black needed was evident after **28...♖xf2**.

White to play

No one wants to play a risky-looking move like 29 g4 without a deep look. But it would gave saved the day after, say, 29...♕d3 30 ♖h5+ ♔g8 31 ♕c8+ ♖f8 32 ♕e6+ with perpetual check.

Instead White played **29 ♕a8+?? ♖f8 30 ♖g5** and **resigned** after **31...♕e4!**.

It is easy to blame White's collapse on his 29th move. But it began with a slight error, 27 ♕xc6.

A move later the only way to preserve an edge was the ungainly 28 ♖b2. He would still have some work to do after 28...♖e8 29 ♗d2 (29 ♗e3?? ♖xe3) ♖e2 30 ♕a8+ ♔h7 31 ♕f3. In between the mild error 27 ♕xc6?! and the fatal 29 ♕a8+?? was a moderate blunder, 28 ♖xb5?.

Swindle Pause

The swindle process is not as inevitable as these examples indicate. Often the player with an advantage recovers from his mistake and finds an excellent move or two. The process becomes a pause. If the pause lasts long enough, the swindle attempt may peter out to a draw.

Uhlmann – Larsen
Beverwijk 1961

Black to play

Black is barely alive and computers tend to disagree about which defeatist policy is best. Some endorse 36...♕g5? 37 ♕xg5 and others prefer 36...a5? (37 ♕f6 ♕e8 38 ♖d2).

Black chose **36...♕e8~**. It threatens ...nothing.

But it plants in White's mind the idea that ...♕g6 or ...♕h5 may work in the near future, when White cannot reply ♖xd7+ and ♕f7+.

There was also the possibility of a sacrifice of h3. For example, 37 ♕d6 ♗xh3 38 ♔xh3?? ♕h5 mate.

But this is a mirage, 37 ♕d6 ♗xh3?? loses in various ways, including 38 ♖c8 (38...♕xc8 39 ♖f7+ and mates).

In fact, after 36...♕e8 White would win with 37 ♕d6 – or with 37 ♕f6, 37 ♖xb7, 37 ♖d2 or just about any solid move.

But he played **37 e5?** and back came **37...♕g6!**.

White to play

By closing the b2-h8 diagonal, White had taken "38 ♖xd7+ ♗xd7 39 ♕f7+ and wins" off the table.

This allowed Black to threaten ...♕g1 mate. There was one defense, **38 ♖c1**.

After a potential swindlee has made a mistake, a good swindler doesn't allow him to recover with easy moves, such as 38...♕h5? 39 ♖f3, when White is still much better.

Bent Larsen was a great swindler and he found: **38...♘c5!**.

Aside from the simple trap (39 ♖xc5?? ♕g1 mate), it prepared to fork four pieces with 39...♘d3.

White to play

Both players were in time trouble. But White was not in the kind of "I must make a move, any move" frenzy that often grips amateurs when they are about to forfeit.

He realized that the fork is a phantom threat and played **39 ♗d4!**.

Then 39...♘d3? would have lost to 40 ♖c7+ ♔h8 41 ♕f6+ (41...♕xf6 42 ♖xf6). Or after 40...♖g7 41 ♖xg7+ ♕xg7 42 ♕e4+.

After **39...b6!** White still had one more move to make in the first time control.

An inexperienced player would be tempted to quickly play 40 ♗xc5 and relax. But White realized that 40 ♗xc5? bxc5 would turn Black's queenside pawns into powerhouses. Black would be better after 41 ♖d2 c4. And 41 ♖xc5?? ♛g1 is that mate again.

White to play

There were also tricks to watch out for such as 40 ♖d2 ♗xh3 41 ♔xh3 ♘e6!.

White did have a solid move in 40 ♛f3, perhaps followed by an equal endgame after 41 ♖g2. Harder to find is 40 ♖b2, followed by ♖g1.

But he played **40 ♛e3??** and after **40...♘b3!** he had time to study the position.

It was too late: He was lost (41 ♖c7+ ♔h8 42 ♖2c2 ♘xd4 43 ♖xd4 ♛g3+ and mates, for instance). He **resigned**.

Shell Shock

Why does a player in a very favorable position blunder twice? The most common reason is that his thinking is thrown off when he realized he made the first blunder.

Toth – Miles
Thessaloniki 1984

1 d4 ♘f6 2 c4 e6 3 ♘c3 ♗b4 4 ♛c2 c5 5 dxc5 0-0 6 ♘f3 ♗xc5 7 ♗f4 b6 8 ♖d1 ♗b7 9 e3 a6 10 ♗e2 ♗e7 11 0-0 d6 12 e4 ♛c7 13 e5 dxe5 14 ♗xe5 ♛c8 15 ♘g5! g6 16 ♘ge4 ♘e8 17 ♘a4! ♘d7 18 ♖xd7! ♛xd7 19 ♘xb6 ♛c6 20 ♘xa8

159

Black to play

After the routine 20...♕xe4 21 ♕xe4 ♗xe4, White will rescue his knight with 22 ♘b6 or trade it off with 22 ♘c7.

Then in addition to his material edge, White would enjoy a two-pawn majority on the queenside and the likely control of the d-file after ♖d1. Winning should be fairly easy.

The same goes for 20...♗xa8. It is not difficult to find 21 ♗f3!. It defends the knight, neutralizes the a8-g2 diagonal and threatens the queen (22 ♘f6+ and ♗xc6).

After 21...♕b6 (or 21...♕c8) 22 ♖d1 f5 23 ♘d2, Black would be a pawn down with little compensation.

With **20...f5!** he forced White to make more difficult choices.

White to play

Black wasn't dreaming of a knight move that allowed 21...♕xg2 mate. Nor was he expecting blunders such as 21 ♗f3? fxe4 and 21 f3? fxe4, when the knight on a8 remains trapped and lost.

White's real choice was between 21 ♘b6 and 21 ♘c7. Both of them would reduce danger on the long diagonal. For example, 21 ♘b6! ♕xb6 allows 22 ♘d2 and a favorable trade of material with 23 ♗f3 or 23 ♕b3.

Black would have better swindling chances with 21...fxe4. But 22 ♘a4 e3 23 f3! (not 23 ♗f3?? ♖xf3 24 gxf3 ♕xf3) keeps White on the road to victory.

Instead, White chose **21 ♘c7?** and after **21...♘xc7** he had to continue **22 ♗xc7** to avoid losing material.

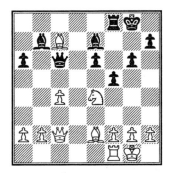

Black to play

Black must have sensed that White had erred. Should he try to induce a second mistake. Specifically, should he gamble with 22...fxe4 ?

It could pay off, after a bishop retreat such as 23 ♗g3, when 23...e3 threatens ...♕xg2 mate. White might fall for 24 ♗f3?? ♖xf3 25 gxf3 ♕xf3 and get mated.

But it would be too easy for him to find 24 f3! and keep a winning advantage. A good swindler doesn't just set traps when his position is improving. Black played **22...♕xc7.**

White to play

He recognized that his bishops have much greater scope than if 21 ♘b6 fxe4 had been played.

White is weak on dark squares. For example, 23 ♘c3 ♗d6 24 g3? ♗c5 (threat of ...♕c6-h1 mate) and 24 h3 ♗c5 25 ♖d1? ♕f4 26 ♗f1 ♗d6.

White played **23 ♘d2.** His position still seemed promising but he had to be concerned after **23...♖d8!**.

He would be worse after 24 &f3 ♕f4 25 &xb7 ♖xd2 26 ♕a4 &c5 because he can't defend f2 (27 &f3? &d6! loses).

And his extra pawn would be lost after 25 ♖d1 &xf3 26 ♘xf3 ♖xd1+ 27 ♕xd1 ♕xc4.

Moreover, Black would be at least equal after 24 ♘f3 g5! and ...g4.

White opted for **24 ♖d1**, which allows him to continue 25 ♘f1 and trade rooks.

Black to play

When your opponent realizes he has thrown away a big advantage, he may be in shell shock. He isn't thinking – or at least, calculating – as he normally would.

That means you should keep pressuring him, as Black did with **24...♕e5!**.

The pressure succeeds after 25 ♘f3 ♖xd1+ 26 &xd1 &xf3 27 &xf3?? ♕e1 mate.

Or, White might be able to defend 27 gxf3 or 25 &f3 &xf3 26 ♘xf3 ♖xd1+ 27 ♕xd1 ♕xb2 28 g3.

And White's advantage would have been minimal after 25 ♘f1 and 25...♖xd1 26 &xd1 ♔f7 27 ♕d2, for example.

But the residual shock of seeing his winning chances dissipate since 18 ♖xd7! had its effect. White replied **25 h3??** then saw he had allowed 25 ...♕xe2. He **resigned** before Black moved.

Your Own Tactics

The vulnerabilities of a swindle that we saw in Chapter Five are often most evident in the second stage of a swindle.

Moller – Staldi
Stockholm 1937

1 d4 ♘f6 2 c4 e6 3 ♘c3 d5 4 &g5 ♘bd7 5 cxd5 exd5 6 e3 &e7 7 &d3 0-0 8 ♕c2 b6 9 ♘f3 &b7 10 &f4 c5 11 0-0 ♖c8 12 ♘e5 g6 13 &h6 ♖e8 14 f4 cxd4 15 exd4 ♘e4 16 &b5 ♘xe5 17 fxe5 &c6 18 &d3 g5 19 &xg5 ♕xg5 20 &xe4 dxe4 21 ♕f2 ♖e7 22 d5 &a8 23 ♘xe4 ♕xe5 24 d6 ♖b7??

If Black appreciated the dangers he would have given up a bit of material, 26...♗xe4 27 dxe7 ♕xe7 and try to draw an endgame after 28 ♖ac1 ♖xc1 29 ♖xc1. He didn't know when to panic.

25 ♘f6+ ♔g7 26 d7 ♖d8 27 ♖ae1? ♕c5 28 ♖e3?

Black to play

White has already overlooked two ways to force resignation.

The first was 27 ♘e8+ (27...♔h8 28 ♕xf7 and 27...♔h6 28 ♕h4+).

The second was 28 ♕xc5 bxc5 29 ♖e7 followed by ♘e8+ and ♖fxf7.

His last move, 28 ♖e3, threatens 29 ♘e8+ ♔h6 30 ♕h4+ ♕h5 31 ♕f4+ g5 32 ♕f6+ and mates.

Black had to play **28...♖bxd7 29 ♘xd7 ♖xd7.**

White to play

This resembles the situation that Black passed up earlier (26...♗xe4). White would have good winning chances after 30 ♕f6+ ♔g8 31 ♕e5 ♕xe5 32 ♖xe5 because 32...♖d2?? 33 ♖e8+ is not playable.

But he may have had doubts about 30...♔h6!.

He could offer a queen trade after 30 ♖e2 and make slow progress after 30...♕d6 31 ♖fe1 ♗b7 32 ♕e3, for example.

The only explanation for **30 ♖ee1??** is that he had stopped looking for Black's tactics.

He lost after **30...♖d2!** because 31 ♕xc5? ♖xg2+ 32 ♔h1 ♖g3+ mates.

Third Result

The reluctance to consider a third result is another common factor in gradual swindles. Look at the next diagram and try to imagine how Black could lose.

Caruana – Dominguez
St. Louis 2017

Black to play

White has just erred and allowed 40...f3!. Then 41 fxg3 ♔f4 and ...♔xf3 would offer chances of winning with the passed c- and h-pawns (42 ♔g2 ♖g5+).

The game continued **40...♔f5? 41 f3!** and a draw was highly likely (41...♔g5 42 ♔h2).

But Black was still better. That changed after **41...♖d5 42 ♔h4! ♔e5 43 ♔xh5 ♔d4+ 44 ♔g4**.

White will win the f-pawn. That should have suggest to Black that it was time to find a draw. One way to do that is 44...c4 45 ♔xf4 c3 and 46 g4 ♖c5 47 ♖d6+ ♖d5 48 ♖c5 ♖c4.

He also had opportunities to draw by giving up his c-pawn in what followed, **44...♔e3 45 ♖e6+ ♔f2 46 ♔xf4 ♔xg2 47 ♖e2+ ♔h3 48 ♖c2 ♖h5**.

White to play

Now on 49 ♔e4 Black would likely have realized the danger of f4-f5. He would have forced a draw with 49...♔g3 50 f4 ♖h4, for example.

But White craftily played **49 ♖c1**. It threatens 50 ♖h1+.

Black should have jettisoned the pawn, 49...♖h4+ 50 ♔e3 ♖a4 because 51 ♖xc5 is another difficult book draw after, for instance, 51...♔g3 52 ♖g5+ ♔h4 53 f4 ♖b4 and ...♖a4-b4.

But Black was not ready to think that way and found himself lost after **49...♔g2?? 50 ♔g4 ♖h8** (or 50...♖d5 51 f4 and 52 f5) **51 ♖c2+ ♔f1 52 ♖xc5 ♔f2** (52...♖g8+ 53 ♖g5) **53 f4 ♔e3 54 f5 ♔d4 55 ♖a5 ♔e4 56 f6**.

In retrospect, he didn't recognize how his winning chances were virtually ended by 41 f3! and that the other two results were much more likely.

Swindlee Meltdown

A player who makes a major error needs time to recover psychologically. The more time the better. Making quick moves invites a tactical meltdown.

Ushenina – Travkina
Sochi 2016

Black to play

White will have more than enough material to win when she adds a third extra pawn. She can take on b4 when she wants.

Black figured that her only chance was to create tactics after trading off the rook at e1, with **37...♖e5!**. Then she might penetrate on the eighth rank with her h6-rook.

If White avoids the trade, 38 ♖d1 – or 38 ♖f1 or even 38 ♖g1 – she would keep an advantage of more than +4.00, according to engines.

Her king can slide away to safety, via c1 and b1, and be perfectly placed. Then she can play ♕xb4 and push her queenside pawns to victory.

But **38 ♖xe5? ♕xe5** created a much different situation.

White to play

Suddenly White can see ways to lose – and lose immediately: 39 ♔c1?? ♛a1+ 40 ♔d2 ♜h1 and ...♛e1 mate or 39 ♛e2?? ♛d4+.

That should sharpen a sense of danger and point toward 39 ♜c1!. Then 39...♛b2+! would force 40 ♜c2.

Black has nothing better than 40...♛e5!, repeating the position. (White would be winning again after 40...♛a1? 41 ♛xf4.)

In the heat of battle, White did not understand what that meant: She could have repeated the position with 39 ♜c1 ♛b2+ 40 ♜c2 ♛e5. That would have reached the time control, when she would be able to decide at her leisure whether to allow a draw by a further repetition or to play to win with an extremely sharp move like 41 ♛xb4.

But she played the immediate **39 ♛xb4,** threatening to start checking on the seventh and eighth ranks or to offer a queen trade with 40 ♛c3. Black had only one good move, **39...♜h1!**.

White to play

Black threatens ...♛e1 mate. Her own king can escape from checks (40 ♛b8+? ♔g7 41 ♛c7+ ♔h6).

The good news for White is that she could still draw. The bad news is that she did not have enough time to find the complex 40 ♗e2!! ♞e4+ 41 ♔d3 ♛xd5+ 42 ♛d4 ♞xf2+ 43 ♔c3 or 40...♛xd5+? 41 ♔c3.

166

To make the time control, she played **40 ♜c1??**. But after **40...♕b2+ 41 ♜c2 ♕a1!** she was lost.

For example, 42 ♕b8+ ♚g7 43 ♕c7+ ♚h6 44 ♜xc5 ♕d4+ 45 ♚c2 ♕xf2+ 46 ♚d3 ♕e3+ 47 ♚c4 ♜c1+.

What happened was worse, **42 ♜xc5?? ♕e1+ 43 ♚c2 ♕xb4** and Black won.

Even a master swindler can become the swindlee if he doesn't have the time to recover psychologically from his first error.

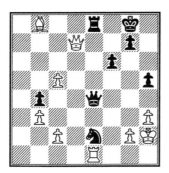

Carlsen – Caruana
Leuven 2016

White to play

White can win if he ever gets to push his c5-pawn. But his immediate concern is that his bishop is attacked.

He could have played 43 ♗g3, so that 43...h4 44 ♗xh4 ♕xh4?? 45 ♕xe8+.

Or 44...♕f4+ 45 ♚h1 ♞g3+ 46 ♗xg3 ♜xe1+ 47 ♗xe1 ♕f1+ 48 ♚h2 ♕xe1. Then 49 ♕d5+ and 50 c6 is a winning queen endgame.

It seemed safe to play **43 ♗d6?** because the bishop is protected. But **43...♜e5!** was a revelation.

White to play

Black threatened 44...♕f4+ and a quick mate. White would lose after 44 ♗xe5? ♕xe5+ 45 ♔h1 ♘g3+.

Magnus Carlsen does not suffer shell shock often. He quickly found **44 ♖f1!**.

But **44...♗g5!** confronted him with a new mate threat.

Carlsen was able to see that 45 ♖f2 would set a minor trap. After 45...♕e3 46 ♖f1 ♘g3? 47 ♖f3! he would win a piece.

But Black can repeat the position with 46...♕e4!.

There was another reason to be concerned about 45 ♖f2. Black can try to divert the bishop from the key diagonal with 45...♖xc5 and 46 ♗xc5 ♕e5+.

This is appealing because if White simplifies with 46 ♖xe2 ♕xe2 47 ♗xc5 he finds that this queen endgame, 47...♕e5+ and 48...♕xc5, favors Black.

(It isn't easy to find in time trouble but 45...♖xc5 46 ♗xc5 ♕e5+ is a draw after 47 ♔h1 ♕a1+ 48 ♖f1! ♕xf1+ 49 ♔h2.)

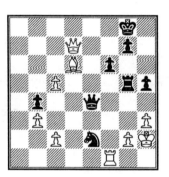

White to play

But Carlsen hadn't recovered from 43 ♗d6? when he played **45 ♖f3?**.

He overlooked **45...♖xg2+! 46 ♔xg2 ♘d4** and soon lost, **47 ♔g1 ♘xf3+ 48 ♔f2 ♘d4** (48...♘h4!) **49 ♕c8+ ♔h7 50 ♕a6 ♕f3+**.

Raising the Stakes

How should the would-be swindler react when his poor position suddenly becomes better? Objectively, he should steer towards a draw. But if his opponent erred once, what is the likelihood he will do it again?

For the would-be swindler the question he can ask is: Is it worth risking a draw in the hopes of stealing a whole point? The answer is often an educated guess. Here it is an educated gamble.

de Firmian – Chernin
Tunis 1985

Black to play

White's position was in sharp decline in the last few moves. He seemed to be the one who was psychologically vulnerable.

Black has a broad choice of possible winning plans:

He could play 34...g4 followed by ...e4 and ...f5. White would have no good answer to ...♖eh6 or ...♕h7, followed by a capture on h2.

Alternatively, Black can win a second pawn with 34...♕h7 followed by 35...♕xc2 or 35...♕xh2+.

Or he could just play 34...exd4. But that gives up the ...e4 option and allows White's bishop to come alive on g2.

Black decided to simplify with **34...♘xd4**. That virtually forced **35 ♗xd4 exd4** and prepared a swap of rooks (...♖xb6).

But 34...♘xd4? threw away much of Black's edge. He underestimated the power of **36 ♕c5!**, a move that can be overlooked when the White bishop sat on c5.

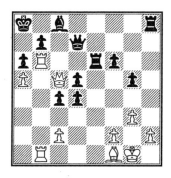

Black to play

Black will have difficulty holding his d4-pawn. Winning would be difficult after **36...♕h7 37 h3 ♕e4** in view of 28 ♖xe6 ♗xe6 29 ♗g2 (29...♕e5 30 ♔f1! and ♖e1). Difficult but not impossible.

169

When a winning position goes bad, a player may begin to distrust his calculation. He may then rely on forcing moves because they are the easiest to calculate. So **37...♖xb6? 38 ♖xb6**.

Now 38...♕xc2? 39 ♕xd5 and Black cannot safely stop ♖xa6+, e.g. 39...♔a7? 40 ♕xd4 ♔a8 41 ♗g2 and White wins.

Or 39...♔b8? 40 ♕d6+ ♔a7 41 ♖xa6+! bxa6 42 ♕b6+ ♔a8 43 ♗g2+.

Black to play

Black suddenly finds himself in the role of defender. He needs to distract White and a good way of doing that was 38...d3 39 cxd3 c3!.

Then 40 ♕xd5? ♕c7! favors Black and 41 ♖xa6+? ♔b8 wins for him. So does 40 ♕xc3? ♗xh3!.

But Black held the d-pawn with **38...♕e4**.

The abrupt change of fortunes gives White reason to raise his expectations. He could try to draw an endgame by regaining pawns.

For example, 39 ♖d6 might lead to 39...d3 40 cxd3 cxd3 41 ♕xd5 ♕xd5 42 ♖xd5 and White should hold.

Even better is 39 ♖xf6 followed by ♖d6. Black couldn't play 39...♗xh3?? because of 40 ♗xh3 ♖xh3? 41 ♖f8+ and mate. And once again 39...♕xc2 40 ♕xd5 sets up that nasty ♖xa6+ threat.

After 39 ♖xf6! White should be at least equal. But he felt the momentum strongly running in his favor and chose **39 ♗g2~**.

Black to play

This was a gamble that would be hard to justify if Black had time to study the position. Then he would have found 39...♛e5!.

He would win outright after 40 ♗xd5?? ♛e1+.

And he might convert his endgame edge after 40 ♕xd5 ♛xd5 41 ♗xd5 c3! because of queening tricks.

For instance, 42 ♖xf6?? d3! 43 cxd3 c2. Or 42 ♖b4 d3! 43 cxd3 ♖d8 44 ♗e4 f5 and ...♖xd3.

Once again, he went for a forcing move, **39...♛e1+? 40 ♔h2**.

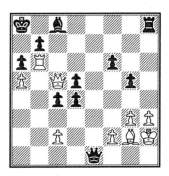

Black to play

Black should still play 40...♛e5!. But the situation is slightly different since 41 ♗xd5! is playable and 41...♖xh3+ 42 ♔g2 would be harmless.

A draw would likely follow 41...♔b8 (42 ♖xa6! ♖xh3+ 43 ♔g2 ♖xg3+! 44 fxg3 ♛e2+ and perpetual check).

But on the final move of the time control he chose **40...♛xf2??** with what appeared to be a decisive threat of 41...♖xh3 mate.

What he overlooked was **41 ♖xa6+!**. It was mate after 41...♔b8 42 ♕d6 or 41...bxa6 42 ♕xd5+.

Regaining Composure

Sometimes ignorance is bliss. Not knowing what you missed can mean not becoming upset. Here is how a grandmaster failed to find a forced checkmate of the world champion. But since he was unaware of it, he wasn't upset – yet.

Carlsen – Ganguly
Doha 2016

Black to play

Black had been winning for several moves. Here he overlooked 36...♖g4+! (37 ♔xg4 ♕g2+ 38 ♔h5 ♕f3 mate).

Fortunately, he didn't learn what he missed until after this speed game was over. He was able to concentrate on the position and still had a winning position after **36...♖xa4 37 h5**.

How should he finish White off? His choice appears limited to two queen moves. One is the messy 37...♕e4.

It is messy because Black would have to calculate not only 38 ♕xe6+ ♔h7 but also 38 ♖d8+ ♗xd8 39 ♕e8+.

He has to be sure he isn't getting mated or allowing perpetual check in the second line, after 39...♔h7 40 g6+ ♔h6. (He isn't: 41 ♕h8+ ♔g5 42 ♕xd8+ ♔xh5!.)

But he chose **37...♕c4** because it threatened checks on g4 and h4 and also averted ♕xe6+.

But 37...♕c4?? was an error in view of **38 ♖d8+!**.

Black to play

This was surprising and prompted **38...♗xd8 39 ♕e8+ ♔h7 40 ♕g6+ ♔g8** draw by perpetual check.

But if Black had regained his composure he would have played 38...♗f8!.

Then 39 h6 would threaten to win. Black could deliver perpetual check (39...♕h4+ 40 ♔g2 ♕g4+) if he didn't see anything stronger.

He might have fallen for 40...♖g4+?? 41 ♔f3! when White turns the tables. There is no more check after 41...♕h3+ 42 ♔e2 and no perpetual check after 41...♖f4+ 44 exf4 ♕xf4+ 45 ♔e2.

Best was 40...♕e4+ 41 ♕xe4 ♖xe4. White would have one last swindle bid, 42 ♔g3. It threatens 43 ♖xf8+! ♔xf8 44 h7.

A draw would be likely after 42...gxh6 43 gxh6 ♔f7 44 h7 ♗g7 45 h8(♕) ♗xh8 46 ♖xh8.

Quiz

21.

Alburt – Dzindzikashvilli
Lone Pine 1980

White to play

The winner of this game would receive $15,000. If it was drawn, the two players would receive $12,500 each.

White could not be sure that 44 ♘xb7! ♔xb7 45 h4 would win because both players queen after 45...a5! 46 h5.

He played **44 ♕d8??** and was stunned by **44...♕e5+!**.

Then 45 ♔h1 ♕e1+ 46 ♔h2 ♕e5+ is perpetual check. So White played **45 g3**.

Black to play

What move would a swindler play?

Vasily Smyslov was not known as a swindler. But he had his moments:

22.

Belavenets – Smyslov
Leningrad-Moscow 1939

Black to play

White made his first major error two moves ago. But he was still expecting to win.

(a) Is there a swindling alternative to **34...♔f6**, the move Black played ?

(b) After **34...♔f6** what would he have done in reply to 35 b7 ?

The game continued **35 ♖e1?** (35 ♗d3! ♖a2 36 ♗e2) **♖dd2 36 ♖g1 g5 37 resigns**.

(c) Why not 36 ♖xe3 ?

Yes, the next position arose in a simultaneous exhibition. And, no, it wasn't Kasparov who gave it. He was only 12 at the time.

23.
Kasparov – Smyslov
Clock simultaneous exhibition, Leningrad 1975

1 e4 e5 2 ♘f3 ♘c6 3 ♗b5 g6 4 d4 exd4 5 ♘xd4 ♗g7 6 ♗e3 ♘f6 7 ♘c3 0-0 8 0-0 ♖e8 9 f3 ♘e5 10 h3 a6 11 ♗e2 d5 12 f4 ♘c4 13 ♗xc4 dxc4 14 ♕f3 c5 15 ♘de2 ♗d7 16 e5 (16 ♗xc5 ♗c6 regains the pawn) **♗c6 17 ♕f2 ♘d7 18 ♗xc5 ♘xc5 19 ♕xc5**

Computers suggest 19...♗f8 and so that 20 ♕xc4 ♕b6+ and 21...♕xb2. But White would be better after 20 ♕e3 (20...♕a5 21 ♘e4).

Black chose **19...♖c8~**. It threatens to discover an attack on the queen with 20...♗xg2 or 20...♗e4/21...♗xc2.

It was risky because after **20 ♖ad1 ♕h4** White might have found 21 ♘d5! with advantage.

21 ♕e3

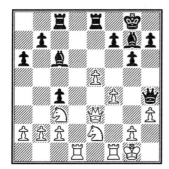

Black to play

The safe move, 21...f6, would have approached equality (22 ♘d4 fxe5 23 ♘xc6).

What is the swindler's choice?

Chapter Nine:
Swindler versus Swindlee

A swindler does not have a monopoly on tactics. Opponents will look for the traps he sets. They will also look for their own tactics.

Here's a case of a future world champion trying to survive a swindle and discovering tactics too late.

Alekhine – Bogolyubov
St. Petersburg 1914

1 e4 e5 2 ♘f3 ♘c6 3 ♗b5 ♗c5 4 c3 ♘ge7 5 d4 exd4 6 cxd4 ♗b4+ 7 ♗d2 ♗xd2+ 8 ♕xd2 a6 9 ♗a4 d5 10 exd5 ♕xd5 11 ♘c3 ♕e6+ 12 ♔f1 ♕c4+ 13 ♔g1 0-0 14 d5 ♖d8?? (14...♘a7!) 15 ♕e1!

Black to play

This retreat wins a piece in view of 15...♘xd5 16 ♗b3.

The key tactical point is that 16...♕c5 17 ♗xd5 ♖xd5? does not work (18 ♕e8+).

Black correctly went into swindle mode. His best try was **15...♗g4!**. He wanted to frighten White with ...♗xf3.

It's largely a bluff: 16 dxc6 ♗xf3 17 gxf3 ♖d6 threatens 18...♖g6 mate but 18 ♕e2 is a simple defense.

Also good was 16 ♘d2 since White can avoid 16...♕f4 17 dxc6? ♖xd2 18 ♕xe7?? ♕xf2 mate. He should win after 17 g3 and 17...♕h6 17 dxc6.

Alexander Alekhine preferred **16 ♗b3** and Black naturally replied **16...♕f4 17 dxc6 ♗xf3**.

Computers say Black would have slim chances after 18 gxf3 ♕g5+ 19 ♔f1.

But White made the human choice of avoiding pawn weaknesses. After **18 ♕xe7 ♗xc6** he faced another choice.

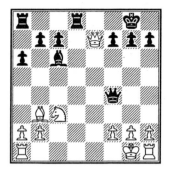

White to play

Black's only tactical resources are trying to target g2 and occupying the seventh rank with his rook.

If Alekhine tries to get queens off the board with 19 ♕e3, it looks risky in view of 19...♕xe3 20 fxe3 ♖d2. But White should have looked further – for his own tactics. Then he might have seen that 21 e4 ♖xb2 favors him after 22 ♖f1!.

That would be followed by a capture on f7 or the forced trade of rooks after 23 ♖f2!.

Instead, Alekhine tried **19 h4** so that his h1-rook can be developed via h3. It can defend g2 after ♖h3-g3.

The drawback was **19...♖d2!** with a threat of 20...♕xf2+.

He would remain lost after 20 ♘e2 and 20...♕g4 21 ♕xf7+ ♔h8 22 ♘g3. But at least his pieces would be active after 20 ...♕f5 21 ♕e3 ♖ad8 (22 ♖h3? ♖8d3 and 22 ♘g3 ♕f6).

White chose a more natural defense, **20 ♖f1**. But it's a blunder because of **20...♖e8!**.

White to play

At this point alarm bells should go off. Alekhine's queen is attacked and when he looks for a retreat square he would see dangerous tactics. That's typically a sign that a swindling process has begun.

White can quickly dismiss the unnatural 21 ♕a3, once he sees that it loses to 21...♖xf2 or 21...♖e1.

A better retreat is 21 ♕c5 because f2 is protected and therefore 21...♖xf2?? 22 ♕xf2 and 21...♖e1?? 22 ♖xe1 fail.

But Alekhine rejected that when he saw that Black could exploit his other tactical resource, the target at g2.

After 21...♗xg2! neither side can improve on perpetual check, 22 ♔xg2 ♕g4+ 23 ♔h2 ♕xh4+.

Alekhine felt his position justified playing for a win. He chose the third queen retreat, **21 ♕g5**.

Black uncorked **21...♖xf2!**. Then 22 ♕xf4 ♖xg2 is a mate and 22 ♖xf2 ♖e1+ only extends the game by one move.

White to play

White finally realized that his position was critical. He could try 22 ♖d1 but 22...♖xg2+ 23 ♕xg2 ♗xg2 is lost.

He took on the role of the swindler with **22 ♗xf7+!**. There are four legal replies.

Two lose (22...♔f8?? 23 ♕c5+ and 22...♔xf7 23 ♕xf4+). One gives White hope (22...♕xf7? 23 ♖xf2! ♖e1+ 24 ♔h2 ♖xh1+ 25 ♔g3!).

But after **22...♔h8!** the win was fairly simple (23 ♗c4 ♕xg5). The game went:

23 ♖d1 ♕xf7 24 ♖d2 h6 25 ♖xf2 ♖e1+ 26 ♔h2 ♕xf2 27 ♕g4 ♗xg2 White resigns.

The moral here is that White began looking for his own tactics too late. If he had checked out 19 ♕e3 ♕xe3 20 fxe3 ♖d2 further he would have seen that 21 e4 and 22 ♖f1! would win. The belated tactical shot, 22 ♗xf7+, was just that: belated.

Until He Runs Out

Once a player adopts the "nothing to lose" attitude, he searches for ways to create threats. Depending on the position and his tactical skill, he may discover remarkable threats.

Then it is up to his opponent to find saving moves. How long must he do this? Until the swindler runs out of threats – or pieces.

Sliwa – Bronstein
Gotha 1957

1 d4 f5 2 g3 g6 3 ♗g2 ♗g7 4 ♘c3 ♘f6 5 ♗g5 ♘c6 6 ♕d2 d6 7 h4 e6 8 0-0-0 h6 9 ♗f4 ♗d7 10 e4 fxe4 11 ♘xe4 ♘d5 12 ♘e2 ♕e7 13 c4 ♘b6? 14 c5! dxc5

Black would be much worse after 14...♘c4 15 ♕c2 d5 16 ♘d2. He is shifting into swindler mode.

15 ♗xc7 0-0 (15...♘xd4 16 ♘d6+ ♔f8 17 ♘f4! is bad) **16 ♗d6 ♕f7 17 ♗xf8 ♖xf8 18 dxc5 ♘d5 19 f4 ♖d8~ 20 ♘2c3 ♘db4~**

White would realizing his winning material advantage more easily after 20...♘xc3 21 bxc3.

Play went **21 ♘d6! ♕f8~ 22 ♘xb7 ♘d4! 23 ♘xd8 ♗b5!**.

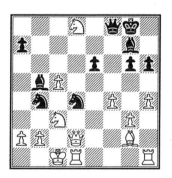

White to play

It is a tribute to Black's ingenuity that he has located his best tactical resources – the mating possibilities on a2 and b3 – even though they were deeply hidden from view at move 19.

He is setting traps. For example, 24 ♘xb5 ♕f5! finally makes a threat (25...♘xa2 mate).

It works after 25 ♘c3?? ♘xa2+ 26 ♘xa2 ♘b3 mate.

Unfortunately, 25 ♕f2 ♕xc5+ 26 ♔d2 or even 25 ♗d5 exd5 26 b3 (or 25...♕xd5 26 ♕xb4) would win.

But there was no reason to look for complications like that when White had **24 ♘xe6!**.

Black to play

Now White would consolidate after 24...♘xe6 25 ♗d5!. Then he has protected the critical a2 square and would be a double Exchange ahead – more than enough to win.

Black's bag of tricks would be empty after 25...♕xc5 26 ♗xe6+ or 25...♘d3+ 26 ♔b1 – or 25...♗d7, the computer-endorsed forms of surrender.

So he found **24...♗d3~**.

The threat is 25...♘xa2+ 26 ♘xa2 ♘b3 mate.

White is so far ahead in material that he could have won with 25 ♕xd3 ♘xd3+ 26 ♖xd3.

That would be the practical choice. White emerges with at least two rooks, a knight and some pawns for the queen after 26...♘xe6 27 ♗d5.

But he was right to feel the game would end faster after **25 ♗d5!**.

Black to play

As in the 24 ♘xe6 ♘xe6 25 ♗d5 line mentioned above, the ♗d5 move protects the key a2-square. Black's threats would be over after 25...♘xe6? 26 ♗xe6+.

White has found enough good moves to win most games. Both 24 ♘xe6! and 25 ♗d5! were splendid defensive stops.

But chess isn't always fair. You have to keep finding good defenses if your opponent keeps coming up with threats. This continues until the would-be swindler runs out of problems to set.

Black wasn't finished yet when he played **25...♕f5~**.

He threatened 26...♕xd5! (27 ♘xd5?? ♘xa2 mate).

After 27 ♘xd4 ♗xd4 he would have reduced his material deficit and could hunt for more tricks.

Play went **26 ♘xd4+ ♕xd5!**.

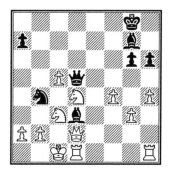

White to play

There were still reasonable moves that would allow Black to continue, such as 27 ♘b3? ♕c4!. Then there would only be one good defense to 28...♘xa2 mate. (But it would eventually win, 28 ♕e1!).

Similarly, 27 ♘de2? ♘xa2+ 28 ♘xa2 ♕xa2 leaves White with one saving move but it may be good enough to win, 29 ♕c3! ♗xc3 30 ♘xc3.

Instead, he ran Black out of attacking pieces. He could have done that with 27 a3!.

He preferred **27 ♘c2!** and the game went **27...♗xc3 28 bxc3 ♕xa2 29 cxb4 resigns**.

Shot for Shot

In the first two examples of this chapter, we saw the player with a great disadvantage resorting to tactics. But the other guy can be the one to begin mixing it up. Then the outcome can depend on who fails to find the next tactical shot.

Smyslov – Vasiukov
Moscow 1961

White to play

White can win if he preserves his two-pawn edge and neutralizes Black's heavy pieces. Those pieces would be too active after 38 ♖c8 ♕b7! and ...♕b1+.

That's why White went for **38 ♕c8!**. It threatens 39 ♕f8 mate.

He could make slow but steady progress in an endgame after 38...♕c8? 39 ♖xc8. For example, 39...♖e4 40 ♖c7+ ♔h6 41 h4 and ♔f1.

Black's best try was **38...♕f3!**. But Vasily Smyslov, one of history's greatest endgame players, could have played 39 ♕b7+ ♕xb7 40 ♖xb7+ and 41 ♖c7 and gotten virtually the same endgame that could have occurred after 38...♕xc8?.

He fell victim to another of the frailties we saw in Chapter Five. He wanted to win quickly, with **39 ♕h8+ ♔h6 40 ♖f8**.

Black to play

He was preparing to close the book with 40...♕e4? 41 ♖f7!.

Better is 40...♕d3 so that 41 ♖f7? falls into a trap, 41...♕d1+ 42 ♔g2 ♕d5+ and ...♕xf7.

But the tactical battle would go on after 40...♕d3 if White found 41 h4!.

That clears h2 so that on 41...♗e7 White would win with 42 ♖f7! ♕d1+ 43 ♔h2! or 41...♕d1+? 42 ♔h2.

However, there is one more improvement: Black would not be losing after 41...♗xh4! because of crazy lines such as 42 ♖f7 ♗xg3 43 ♕f8+! ♔h5 44 ♖xh7+ ♔g5 (and not 43 ♕xh7+?? ♔g5 when Black wins).

In any case, Black chose **40...♕b7** and White replied **41 h4!**.

Black to play

White was still trying to win tactically, 41...♗e7?? 42 ♖f7 (42...♕b1+ 43 ♔h2 as we saw before).

With Black's queen on b7 rather than d3, 41...♗xh4 appears stronger because 42 ♖f7 is not possible. And 42 gxh4 ♖xc2 is quite lost.

But White can reach a drawable endgame after 42 ♖b8 ♕f3 43 ♕f8+.

Black's queen placement also gives him a way to play to win, with **41...♗e3!**.

This set a simple trap (42 fxe3?? ♕g2 mate) but also a more complex one, 42 ♖b8? ♕f3 43 ♕f8+ ♕xf8 44 ♖xf8 ♗c5!.

In addition, Black would be the only one with winning chances after 42 ♘xe3 ♖e1+ 43 ♘f1 ♕b5.

Then White can draw a queen endgame, provided that he sidesteps traps: 44 ♔g2 ♕xf1+ 45 ♔f3 ♕h1+ 46 ♔g4 ♖e4+ 47 ♖f4! ♕d1+ 48 ♔h3! (48 f3?? ♕d7 mate) ♖xf4 49 gxf4 ♕f3+.

White to play

White could try to calculate all that. But so much better is trying to find one last tactical shot of your own. White played **42 ♖f5!**.

One threat is 43 ♕f8+ ♕g7 44 ♘xe3 gxf5 45 ♘xf5+. The other is 43 g4 and 44 ♖h5+! gxh5 45 ♕f6 mate.

The main point is that 42...gxf5 43 ♕f6+ ♔h5 is more than perpetual check (44 ♕xf5+ ♔h6 45 ♕f6+ ♔h5 46 g4+! ♔xg4 47 ♘e3+ and wins).

Black had only one good reply, **42...♖xc2**, and so did White, **43 ♕f8+ ♕g7 44 ♖h5+! gxh6 45 ♕d6+ draw**. It is perpetual check, 45...♕g6 46 ♕f8+ ♕g7 47 ♕d6+.

This was a magnificent series of tactical ideas. Was there anything "swindly" in it?

Yes, but Black missed it. After the faulty bid to win with 39 ♕h8+??, Black could have turned the tables with 40...♕d5!.

White to play

That would have stopped 41 ♖f7, as 40...♕b7?? did.

But this time 41 h4 loses to 41...♗e7. The attacked knight can't move (41 ♘b4?? ♖e1 mate).

And 41 ♖c8 ♕f5! would threaten 42...♕xf2+ and win (42 ♕d4 ♕xc8 or 42 f4 ♗e7 and ...♗c5+).

"Only Moves"

When the tactical level is at its highest, a game can become a battle of "only" moves. The swindler comes up with the one move that keeps his hopes alive. His opponent finds the one good reply. The struggle continues until someone errs.

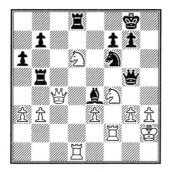

Kogan – Benjamin
South Bend 198

Black to play

White's threats to capture on f7 or b5 give him a decided advantage. Computers look at 32...♗d5 and eventually find that Black is losing after 33 ♕c7.

Black found the best practical try, **32...♖xd6! 33 ♖xd6 ♖c5**.

He had seen a mating pattern with ...♖c1-h1 as well as counterplay after 34 ♕e2 ♖c3.

White can rule out that ...♖c3 idea with 34 ♕d4. Then on 34...♖c1 35 ♘g2 he would be threatening 36 ♖xf6 and 37 ♕xe4.

But 35...♘g4+! 36 hxg4 ♕xg4 is far from a White win.

In time pressure, it was hard to pass up **34 ♖d8+ ♔h7 35 ♕xf7**. After all, it wins a pawn, makes a threat and – perhaps most important – gets closer to the end of the control at move 40.

Black to play

White is ready to end matters with 36 ♕f8! and 37 ♕h8 mate. Black had a single good move, **35...♖c1!**, and it threatened ...♖h1 mate.

Only after the game was it clear that Black's king was safer than White's. White can survive with "only" moves, 36 ♖g2! ♗xg2 37 ♕f8!.

That seems to win, in view of 37...♔h6 38 ♕h8+ ♘h7 39 ♖d6+.

But Black also has an "only" move, 37 ...♘g4+!.

Then 38 hxg4? falls into a trap, 38...♕h6+ 39 ♘h5 ♖h1+! 40 ♔xg2 ♕c6+ 41 ♕f3 ♖g1+!.

Instead, White can escape with 38 ♔xg2! since Black only has perpetual rook checks at c2 and c1.

Instead, White played **36 ♘g2??**.

Black to play

This might be called the second step of a two-step swindle, the first being 35 ♕xf7?. White was lost after **36...♕xe3!** (37 ♘xe3 ♖h1 mate or 37 ♖xf6 ♕g1 mate).

There was no perpetual check after 37 ♖d7 ♘xd7 38 ♕h5+ ♕h6. There was an "only" move, the only alternative to resigning, **37 ♖dd2**.

And there was only one good reply, 37...♗xg2 and it should have won. For example, 38 ♖xg2 ♕e1 or 38 ♔xg2 ♕e4+! 39 ♖f3 ♕e1!.

However, Black didn't want to give away that great bishop. He played **37...♗c6??**. There was no threat, other than a belated 38...♗xg2!.

So **38 ♖de2! ♕h6** was quickly played.

White to play

White could see the threat of 39...♘g4 mate. There are two ways to avert it and one of them, 39 ♖xf6? ♕xf6, would only draw.

The other, 39 ♕e6!, would win. But to play it White would have to see that after 39...♗d7 he would only have one good reply – the winning 40 ♖xf6!.

Instead, White met the ...♘g4+ mate threat with **39 ♖f4**, which made its own threat, 40 ♖h4.

Black quickly replied **39...♗d5** and the game ended with **40 ♕e7 ♕xh3+! 41 ♔xh3 ♖h1 mate**.

Two of White's last three moves and one of Black's last three moves were blunders: 39 ♖f4?? allowed 39...♕xh3+!. And 39...♗d5?? allowed 40 ♖xf6!, when a draw is likely after 40...♗xf7 41 ♖xh6+. Tartakower was proven right once more.

A Swindlee Miracle

Swinders have won miraculous games from positions that seemed beyond hopeless. Here is the other side: a miraculous reverse at the very end of what should have been a great swindle.

Reshevsky – Savon
Petropolis 1973

White to play

Black's three passed pawns and bishop are far superior to the clumsy white rook.

Computers like 28 ♘b3 despite 28...♕a3!. Then 29 ♘d4 ♕a1+ and mates. And 29 ♗d1 c2 is lost.

The reason they like 28 ♘b3 ♕a3 is 29 g4!, which creates luft while attacking the bishop.

But an appropriate finish would be 29...♗xg4! 30 ♗xg4 ♕xb3 31 d6 ♕b1+ 32 ♔g2 c2 White resigns.

Instead, White played **28 ♘e4~**. It's a good try in a bad position and should have lost quickly after 28...♗xe4. Then the c-pawn rolls on after 29 ♖xe4 c2 30 ♕d2 ♕c5 31 ♖e1 ♗b2.

But 29 ♗xe4 would halt the c-pawn. It was harder to see that then 29...♗d4! wins because 30 ♖e1 walks into 30...♗b6! and the queen is trapped (31 ♕xa6 ♗xf2+ and ...♕xa6).

The first major Black error of the game was **28...♕a3?**. His win was not gone but would have become more difficult after 29 ♖e1.

White preferred **29 ♘xc3~ ♗xc3 30 ♕d8+ ♔g7 31 g4**.

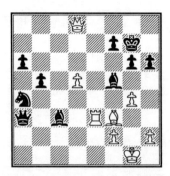

Black to play

Suddenly White seems to have counterchances from ♖e8-g8+.

But Black is winning in lines such as 31...♕a1+ 32 ♔g2 ♗d4! 33 ♖e8 ♗d3!. There is only one check for White, 34 ♖g8+ ♔h7.

Black may have had doubts about giving up his material edge after 33 gxf5 ♗xe3 34 fxe3.

In time pressure, he relied on moves that were easy to calculate, **31...♕c1+ 32 ♔g2 ♗f6**.

Then 33 ♕b8 ♗d7! would begin to close the curtains because ♖e8 is ruled out and the d-pawn's advance is blocked.

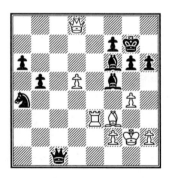

White to play

Black didn't give **33 ♕d6!** enough attention. It blocks the d-pawn but creates a much more serious last-rank threat, ♖e8 and ♕f8+, than he faced from ♖e8-g8+ earlier.

He had no time to calculate a "computer" continuation such as 33...♗d3 34 ♖xd3 ♘b2. (Without a computer, who would trust that?)

Black naturally played **33...♗b1** and the next moves, **34 ♖e8 ♕c5 35 ♕b8**, were virtually forced on both sides.

Black must have begun to regret his failure to calculate more deeply at move 31. Now 35...♕b6 36 ♖g8+ ♔h7 37 ♕e8! and the tactics are running in White's favor.

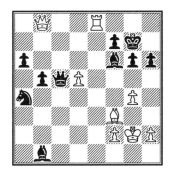

Black to play

Black tried to get his knight back into play, **35...♘b6**.

Chances would be close to even after 36 ♖g8+ ♔h7 37 ♖f8 ♗g7 38 ♖xf7 ♘c4. White could be a shade better after 37 ♕e8! ♕c7 (37...♕e7?? 38 ♖h8+!) 38 ♖f8 ♗g7 39 ♖xf7 ♕d6.

Since Black had one minute to play five moves and reach the time control, White set a trap with **36 ♖h8**.

His threat of ♕g8 mate means Black must move his f6-bishop. If it stays on the long diagonal, he loses, 36...♗c3? 37 ♕g8+ ♔f6 39 ♖h7! with the threats of 40 ♖xf7+ or 40 ♕g7+.

This was a no-risk trap because if the bishop had gone to h4 or g5, White could take a perpetual check draw with 37 ♕g8+ ♔f6 38 ♕d8+ ♔g7 39 ♕g8+.

Considering how lost he was at move 27, that has to be considered a triumph. His move prompted **36...♗e7**.

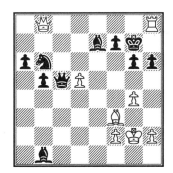

White to play

189

Now on 37 ♕e5+ Black could have used his remaining seconds to make a crucial decision. With 37...♗f6 he would offer to repeat the position, 38 ♕b8 ♗e7, and accept a draw. Or he could take a risk with 37...f6?! 38 ♕b8.

There was also 37 ♕g8+ ♔f6 38 ♖h7 to consider. It's shocking but not only is there no mate after 38...♘xd5!, Black would have the superior winning chances.

What he didn't appreciate was **37 ♖g8+!**. The swindle would be nearly complete after 37...♔f6 38 ♕f4+ ♗f5 39 gxf5.

It *should* have been complete after **37...♔h7?? 38 ♕e8!**.

If Black had enough time, he would have resigned. He would have seen that he cannot delay mate for more than five moves.

Out of inertia, Black played **38...h5**. Next came **39 ♕xf7+ ♔h6**.

White to play

A swindler lives and dies with tactics. The natural continuation is 40 ♖h8+, forcing 40...♔g5.

Then White can consider 41 gxh5. It wins.

If he takes more time he would find a mate (41 h4+! ♔xh4 42 ♖xh5+! gxh5 43 ♕xh5 mate).

Or he would have found the most forcing line, 40 g5+! ♗xg5 41 ♖h8 mate or 41...♔xg5 42 h4+! and mate next.

But a miracle happened – and miracles aren't the exclusive property of swindlers. White played **40 ♕xg6+??**.

He thought it was mate. But he had to resign after **40...♗xg6!**.

Quiz

Now let's see if you can avoid being swindled.

24.

Minasian – Adams
Debrecen 1992

White was lost after 14 moves:

1 b3 e5 2 ♗b2 ♘c6 3 e3 d6 4 ♗b5 ♗d7 5 ♘e2 a6 6 ♗xc6 ♗xc6 7 0-0 ♕g5 8 f3 ♘f6 9 c4 d5 10 ♘bc3 0-0-0 11 a4 dxc4 12 bxc4 ♗c5 13 ♔h1 ♗xe3 14 ♗c1 ♗xd2

But he found a way to complicate, **15 ♘b5! ♔b8 16 ♘ed4 ♗xc1 17 ♘xc6+ bxc6 18 ♕b3~ cxb5 19 axb5 ♕e3 20 ♕a4 ♗b2 21 ♕xa6 ♗xa1 22 ♖xa1**.

Black to play

How did Black avoid being swindled?

Chapter Ten:
Royal Swindles

There is a special category of swindles involving unique situations of kings. These are perpetual check, stalemate and king marches. Kings are often the victims of the most remarkable turnabouts. This includes positions with very little material besides kings.

Papin – Nechepurenko
St. Petersburg 2008

White to play

Black threatens 62...♕xg4. If he can play that, White's only hope would be perpetual check.

For example, 63 ♕xb5 ♕d1+ 64 ♔g2 ♕c2+ 65 ♔f3 ♕xa2?? allows a saving check after check, starting with 66 ♕d7+ or 66 ♕e5+.

Instead, Black could win with 63...♕f3+ and ...f3, among other ways, e.g. 64 ♔g1 ♕e3+ 65 ♔f1 f3 or 65 ♔h2 f3.

White's only chance was to create counterplay with **62 a4!**.

Black can still win with some careful checks, 62...♕d3+ 63 ♔f2 ♕g3+ 64 ♔f1 ♕f3+.

Then 65 ♔g1 ♕xg4 is with check.

And 65 ♔e1 ♕xg4 66 ♕b7+ loses after 66...♔f6 because a queen check on b6 or c6 goes into a simple pawn endgame.

After 67 ♕c6+ ♕e6+! 68 ♕xe6+ ♔xe6 69 a5 ♔d6, and Black is "in the square."

However, Black thought **62...bxa4 63 bxa4 ♕xg4?** was a safer way to win.

White to play

He misjudged **64 ♕b7+!**. He can't escape perpetual check because he can't safely use his queen to block checks.

For example, 64...♔g6 65 ♕c6+ ♔h5 allows 66 ♕h1+. The point is that 66...♕h4?? 67 ♕xh4+ and 68 a5 reveals that White has the faster pawn.

But Black chose **64...♔f6 65 ♕b6+ ♕e6**. He counted on 66 ♕xe6+ ♔xe6 67 a5 ♔d6, as we saw above.

What he overlooked was **66 a5!** when there was nothing better than resigning.

It was another two-stage blunder, 63...♕xg4? threw away a win and 65...♕e6?? blundered away a draw.

Perpetual Pain

When a large material imbalance results in perpetual check, the most common cause is carelessness. But in some cases, the carelessness is induced by a swindler's skill.

I. Sokolov – Sakaev
Neum 2000

Black to play

The pinned rook is lost. Minimizing moves suggested by engines (such as 37...b3) are computer-dumb. White would win the endgame after 38 ♕e8+ ♚h7 39 ♕xe5 ♕xe5 40 ♗xe5.

Instead of resigning, Black chose **37...g4~**. White knew enough to ask "What's the point?"

He would look at 38 ♕e8+ ♚h7 39 ♕xe5 and realize 39...♕c6+ sets a trap.

He cannot escape perpetual check after 40 ♚h2 ♕c2+! because ♚h3 is illegal thanks to 37...g4.

But White can end the checks with 38 ♚g1!. There would be nothing to calculate further.

An alternative is a bit more complex, 38 ♕e8+ ♚h7 39 ♕xe5 ♕c6 40 e4!, so that 40...♕c1+ 41 ♗g1.

White chose **38 ♕f5** because the queen watches c2, a key checking square.

Black made one last try, **38...♕c6+**.

White to play

Now 39 ♚h2 would all but end the game.

However, White saw another finish – 39 ♚g1 ♕c1+ 40 ♕f1. The game would end with 40...♕c7 41 ♕a1 resigns.

But after **39 ♚g1??** he was stunned by **39...♚g8!**.

Incredibly, it forces perpetual check. For example, 40 ♕xe5 ♕c1+ and 41...♕c2+.

If the rook isn't taken, Black would be winning (40 ♕xg4+ ♖g5).

The game ended with **40 ♗xe5 ♕c1+ 41 ♚g2 ♕d2+ draw** (42 ♕f2? ♕d5+).

194

Not Just Checks

When one player begins checking, the opponent has to weigh whether he can safely play to win or should judiciously allow a draw. Kings can be checked but they can also be mated.

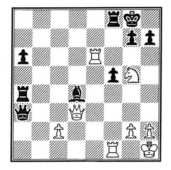

Hou Yifan – Le Quang Liem
Gibraltar 2012

White to play

White had been worse for much of the middlegame. Now she recognized a hidden tactical weakness on Black's first rank.

White could have tried a neat trap, 33 c3. It has two possible payoffs:

First, Black would be mated after 33...♕xc3?? 34 ♕xf5!.

Second, he loses after 33...♗xc3 34 ♖e8! (34...♖xe8 35 ♕d5+ mates, or 34...h6! 35 ♕xf5!).

The best answer to 33 c3 is 33...h6!. Then a draw is likely, after 34 ♖e8 hxg5 35 ♖xf8+ ♕xf8 36 cxd4 ♖a3. Or 34...♖xe8 35 ♕xf5 hxg5 36 ♕f7+.

Instead, 33 ♕e2! threatened 34 ♖e8. The best defense was to exploit White's own first-rank problem with 33...♗f6. Then 34 ♖xf5? ♕c1+ 35 ♖f1 ♖a1! and wins.

The fair outcome of 33 ♕e2! ♗f6! is a drawn endgame: 34 ♖e8! ♗xg5 35 ♕e6+ ♔h8 36 ♕f7! ♗e7! 37 ♖xf8+ ♗xf8 38 ♖xf5 h6 39 ♕xf8+ ♕xf8 40 ♖xf8+ ♔h7.

Black may have felt he deserved more and played **33...h6**.

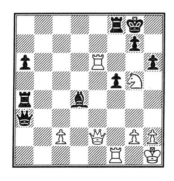

White to play

It made sense because 34 ♖e8? loses to 34...hxg5 35 ♕e6+ ♔h7.

But White had **34 ♖xh6! gxh6 35 ♕e6+**.

She could count on **35...♔g7** because 35...♔h8?? 36 ♕xh6+ allows mate.

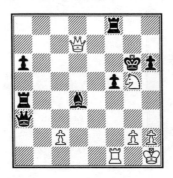

White to play

This position was relatively easy to calculate once she saw 34 ♖xh6 because Black's replies are forced and White has to look for checks. Otherwise she would be a rook down and lost.

That meant **36 ♕d7+**. Black could not play 36...♔h8?? or 36...♔g8?? because of ♕h7 mate. Also suicidal was 35...♔f6?? 36 ♖xf5+.

Black had to play **36...♔g6** and White had her first choice since 34 ♖xh6.

Among the options were queen checks on e6 and h7.

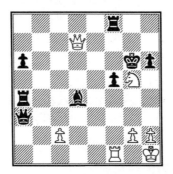

White to play

It appeared there was a good chance for perpetual check in either case, e.g. 37 ♕e6+ ♔xg5 38 h4+! forces 38...♔h5 and then 39 ♖xf5+ ♖xf5 40 ♕xf5+ ♔h4 and checks at f4 and f5.

But as we've seen, in time pressure, a less forcing move tends to have better chances of confusing and opponent. That explains **37 ♘e6!**.

White threatens checks on f4 and f8 (38 ♘xf8+ ♕xf8 39 ♕xa4) and possibly a capture on d4.

Black could see that 37...♖f6?? allows mate after 38 ♘f4+ ♔g5 39 ♕g7+ (or 38 ♕g7+).

In the heat of battle it was harder to evaluate 37...♖f7.

White to play

White can try for perpetual check with her knight or go for more than a draw with 38 ♕e8.

After the game it became clear that 38 ♘f4+! was best. Neither side can improve on 38...♔g7 39 ♘h5+ ♔g6 40 ♘f4+. Or 39...♔g8 40 ♕e8+ ♖f8 41 ♕g6+ (and not 40...♕f8?? 41 ♕xa4).

There were also ways for Black to lose, such as 38...♔f6?? 39 ♘h5+ ♔g6 40 ♕e6+ ♗f6 41 ♕xf5 mate and 40...♔xh5 41 ♕xf7+.

But instead of 37...♖f7, Black chose **37...♗c5??**. It was the kind of move that even a great player makes when he is bewildered.

Its chief benefit was to set a trap, 38 ♘f4+?? ♖xf4 and 39 ♖xf4 ♕c1+.

White would have at least perpetual check after 38 ♘xf8+ ♗xf8 39 ♕xf5+. She might even consider 38 ♘xc5.

But there was better: **38 ♕g7+ ♔h5 39 ♘xf8 ♗xf8 40 ♕f7+**. Black **resigned** in view of 40...♔g5 41 ♖xf5+ or 40...♔h4 41 ♕f6+ ♔g4 42 ♕g6+ ♔h4 43 g3+.

King as Hero

So far we've considered kings as victims, of perpetual check and surprise mates. But in an endgame a king is typically a hero. He becomes a powerful attacker of enemy pawns and a shepherd of his own pawns as they advance.

But when is it safe for a king to become that hero? There is no official end point of a middlegame and starting point for an endgame. That leaves a fuzzy boundary which often provides the basis for "lucky" results.

Torre – Tukmakov
Leningrad 1987

White to play

A pawn up, Black would have good winning chances if he can trade rooks, less so if only queens are traded.

His last move, of his queen from e6, was good because it threatens to win immediately with 47...d4+!.

After **47 ♕b8+!** he could see that a rook endgame, 47...♕c8 48 ♕xc8+ ♖xc8 49 ♖b5 (49...d4 50 ♖d5), would be difficult to win.

The best winning try was **47...♔h7**. In heavy-piece endgames like this, a king can sometimes make a daring march to victory.

The king would become a hero after 48 ♖b7+?? ♔h6 and now 49 ♕h8+ ♔g5 50 ♕d8+ ♔f4 51 ♕h4+ ♔f3.

Thanks to his king, Black is the one threatening mate, beginning with 52...♖c1+.

If White tries 48 ♕b7+ ♕xb7 49 ♖xb7+ instead, this rook endgame is much more promising than the one that could have arisen from 48...♕c8 49 ♕xc8+.

The difference is Black's improved king position, 49...♔h6 50 ♖b5 ♔g5! 51 ♖xd5 ♔f4 (or 51...♔h4). Black is threatening 52...♔g3! and ...♖c1 mate.

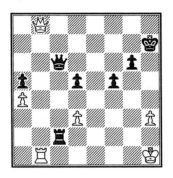

White to play

White found a better check in **48 ♕a7+!**.

It was easy to see that 48...♔h8?? 49 ♖b8+ and 48...♕c7?? 49 ♖b7 were verboten.

When Black allowed 47 ♕b8+ he tried to see what would happen after **48...♔h6 49 ♕e3+**.

When this position arose on the board, it was easy to sort out a loss (49...g5?? 50 ♖b6) and a draw (49...♔h7 50 ♕e7+ ♔h6 51 ♕h4+, with perpetual check).

But **49...♔h5** maintained his winning hopes. He would win another rook endgame after 50 ♕d4 ♕c3! 51 ♕xc3 ♖xc3.

And note the triumphal completion of the king march: If 51 ♕xd5? (instead of 51 ♕xc3) Black would win with 51...♕c7, threatening ...♕h2 mate. Then 52 ♕f3+ ♔h4 53 ♔g1 ♕g3+ 54 ♕xg3+ ♔xg3.

So, play went **50 ♕f3+! ♔h4!** and White had nothing better than **51 ♕f4+**.

Black to play

Now 51...♔h5 52 ♕f3+ leads to perpetual check.

White must take the draw because a mate threat, 52 ♖g1??, allows mate, 52...d4+!.

But what Black had in mind when he began his king march up the h-file was **51...♔xh3**.

Then after 52 ♕h6+ ♔g4 53 ♖g1+ ♔f3 his king is astonishingly safe.

For example, 54 ♕h3+ ♔e2 55 ♖g2+ (better 55 ♕f1+) ♔d1 56 ♖g1+ ♔d2 and Black is close to winning.

All very neat. But after **52 ♖f1!** Black resigned before ♖f3+.

Desperate Kings

King marches become more of a swindler's weapon when, once you have "nothing to lose."

Then an advancing king can be a dramatic way to grab your opponent's attention. Instead of cashing in the material he won, he begins to look for a checkmate.

He may find it. Some king marches are suicidal. But if your position is truly lost, getting mated is no worse than resigning.

N. Weinstein – Suttles
Chicago 1973

White to play

To avoid a lost endgame, Black moved his king from g8 to e6 in the last five moves. That handed White a familiar problem. He has too many ways to win.

One is 34 h4. Then 34...gxh4 35 f4! threatens 36 f5+ and leads to a mating attack after 35...exf4 36 ♖e1+ or 35...e4 36 ♖d4.

There's a somewhat more elaborate win in 34 ♕g8+ ♔e7 35 ♕g7+ so that 35...♔e8 loses to 36 ♖d3 and ♖h3-h8 mate.

But White felt there must be something simpler and chose **34 ♖d8**.

He was right. After **34...♘b7** he had 35 ♖f8!. It threatens 36 ♖xf6+! ♔xf6 37 ♕h6+ and ♕xc6. There are various ways to finish after 35...♘d6, including 36 ♕g6.

But **35 ♖c8** was sufficient. Computers say Black should defend his c7-pawn with 35...♕d7? and play out 36 ♕xd7+.

Black preferred **35...♔d6~**.

White to play

White had played nearly a dozen forcing moves in a row. He could stop to make luft, 36 h3. But he wanted to push matters head. Both 36 ♖f8 and 36 ♕g6 are still strong and so is 36 ♕f5.

He chose **36 ♕g7** because Black cannot simultaneously defend the f6- and c7-pawns (36...♔e6 37 ♖xc7).

To his horror he saw that **36...♕xc2!** would refute 37 ♕xf6+?? with 37...♔d7 because both ...♔xc8 and a first-rank mate are threatened.

It was hard to believe: The win was gone because belatedly making luft with 37 g3 would allow perpetual checks at b1 and e4 and f5, while 37 h3 allows perpetual checks at c1 and f4.

He played **37 ♕f8+**.

Black to play

Black is ready to change his thinking: He knew by now that 36 ♕g7?? was a blunder. Would White make another?

Many players in Black's shoes would be so relieved at the turn of events that they would play 37...♔d7. White has nothing better than perpetual check, 38 ♕e8+ ♔d6 39 ♕f8+.

If Black is a bit more ambitious he could play 37...♔c6. That revives the 38 ♕xf6+?? ♔d7 trap.

If 38 ♕e8+ instead, he can allow perpetual check with 38...♔d6 or play for more with 38...♔b6. If White doesn't trust what is happening he could be the one allowing perpetual check, with 39 h3 ♕c1+ 40 ♔h2 ♕f4+ 41 ♔g1 ♕c1+.

In true swindler spirit Black chose **37...♔d5!**. His king is quite safe because ♖d8+ is not possible.

Play went **38 ♕g8+ ♔d4~** and White regained his composure. His **39 g3** was a tacit draw offer: 39...♕b1+ 40 ♔g2 ♕e4+ leads to perpetual check.

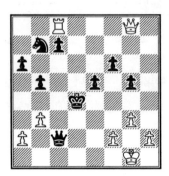

Black to play

But Black wanted the tide to keep turning. He chose **39...♘d6!**. His king is becoming an aggressor.

After 40 ♕d8 Black can play 40...♔d3! and set a trap:

41 ♖xc7?? loses to 41...♕b1+ 42 ♔g2 ♔e2! because of the ...♕f1 mate threat. White also loses after 41 ♕xc7?? ♘xc8.

It made sense to get the rook away from potential ...♘xc8 captures so White played **40 ♖d8?**.

The swindle would have been close to complete after 40...♕b1+ 41 ♔g2 ♕e4+ and then 43 ♔g1 ♔d3! sets up a winning 44...♔e2! followed by 45...♕b1+ 46 ♔g2 ♕f1 mate.

Or 43 ♔h3 ♔d3! and 44...♔e2 (or 44 ♕e6 ♕f3).

But fortune changed sides once again, **40...♔c3? 41 ♕d5!**.

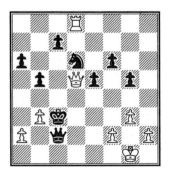

Black to play

Black has lost his chance to use his king in a mating attack (...♔d3-e2). He also lost his perpetual check mechanism. White would win after 41...♕b1+ 42 ♔g2 ♕e4+ 43 ♕xe4 ♘xe4 44 ♔f3 (44...♘d6 45 h4).

But Black has new ways to play to win. One is 41...♕e2 with the idea of 42...♘e4!.

He preferred **41...♔b2~** so he could pick off queenside pawns with his king.

This is risky because White's kingside pawns may be faster, e.g. 42 ♕f3 e4 43 ♕xf6+ ♔xa2 44 b4! followed by ♕xg5 and h2-h4-h5.

White chose **42 ♖a8??** because 42...♔xa2 43 ♖xa6+ would finally get him the king attack he had been seeking for a dozen moves.

But **42...♘e4!** was fatal. White **resigned** after 43 ♔g2 ♕xf2+ 44 ♔h3 f5 45 ♕xe5+ ♔b1.

Transitional Monarch

The way that a king can switch from being the hunter to the hunted (or vice versa) is a standard feature of many dramatic swindles. Here's another striking case.

Black is lost because of her weak pawns. With nothing to lose, she lures White into a search for a forced mate.

Gunina – Arabidze
European Women's
Championship 2014

Black to play

White threatens to win the h7-pawn with 53 ♕h8+. That pawn, or the other weak one at d5, would fall after 52...♘d8 53 ♕a8!.

There is also a trick fork, 53...h6 54 ♕a7 and 55 ♕xb6 ♕xb6 56 ♘xd5+.

Black chose a move-to-confuse, **52...♘e7**.

It does not stop 53 ♕h8+ but it gave White something to think about. She chose **53 ♕f8+!**.

After **53...♔g5** she had three attractive options: the check on g7, the subtle 54 ♕f7 and the subtler 54 ♘d3.

White to play

The last two options would win quickly by threatening mate. For example, 54 ♕f7 threatens 55 ♘e6+ ♔g4 56 ♔g2 and 57 f3+.

The best Black might hope for is a losing endgame after, such as 54 ...♘g6 55 ♕xd5.

But the shock value of Black's king advance prompted **54 ♕g7+ ♘g6.**

A queen ending, 55 ♕xh7 ♘xf4 56 exf4+ ♕xf4, is close to a win after 57 ♕g8+ and ♕xd5. So is 55 ♕g8 and ♕xd5. Or 55 ♔g2, with a threat of 55 ♘h3+.

But the dance of the black king convinced White there was more immediate punishment, so **55 ♘h3+ ♔g4.**

There was no mate. But her winning chances would have remaining good after 56 ♕xh7. Instead, she opted for **56 ♕h6.**

Black to play

The mate finally seems to be near because of 57 ♘g5! and 58 f3+. Or 57 f4! and 58 ♘f2+.

But 56 ♕h6?? has handed Black the advantage after **56...♕h2!.** Suddenly Black's king is a powerful piece, supporting ...♕xh3+.

White could have gone desperate with 57 ♕g5+ ♔xh3 58 ♕xf5+ and 59 ♕xd5.

Having been swindled since 52...♘e7, White tried to become a swindler with **57 f3+**, based on 57...♔xf3?? 58 ♘g1+

Then came **57...♔g3 58 ♕g5+**.

Black to play

This set another simple trap, 58...♔xh3?? allows 59 ♕xf5+ and mate.

But it was evident that the swindle bid had failed after **58...♔xf3.** On 59 ♘g1+ Black plays 59...♔e4 and is winning, e.g. 60 ♘e2 ♕h3+ and ...♕xe3(+) or 60 ♕f6 ♘h4.

White may have hoped for perpetual check after **59 ♕xf5+ ♔xe3**.

But checks only drive the black king closer to munching on queenside pawns, e.g. 60 ♕e6+ ♔d2! 61 ♕e1+ ♔c2.

White gambled on **60 ♘f2~**.

Black to play

It was a gamble because of a knight fork. It was not the fork that White was threatening (61 ♘g4+).

It was the fork she allowed, 60...♕g2+! 61 ♔xg2 ♘h4+ and 62...♘xf5 with an easily won knight endgame.

But there was one more twist. Black played **60...♔xd4??**.

White could have tried for a draw with 61 ♕f6+ ♕e5 62 ♕xb6+ (or delivered mate after 61...♔c5?? 62 ♘d3).

But he won the queen with **61 ♕d3+! ♔c5** (61...♔e5 62 ♘g4+) **62 ♕c2+ ♔d4 63 ♕b2+! resigns** (before 64 ♘d3+ and ♕xh2).

Stalemate

Through the ages, stalemate has often seemed the most unfair of unfair results. A player outplays his opponent so much that his extra material accidentally denies the opponent a single legal move.

But good swindlers know that stalemate frequently comes about by design rather than accident.

Matulovic – Suttles
Palma de Mallorca 1971

Black to play

Black had been lost for more than 30 moves. With **70...♔a6!** and **71 ♘c7+ ♔a7** he seemed to be trying to end the game quickly.

White needs his king on the queenside so he played the natural **72 ♔f2??**.

He didn't notice that Black's only legal moves are with his rook, such as **72...♖d2+**.

Then 73 ♔e3 ♖d3+! 74 ♔xd3 is stalemate. So is 74 ♔e4 ♖xb3! 75 ♖xb3.

The game ended with **73 ♔e1 ♖e2+! 74 ♔f1 ♖f2+ 75 ♔g1 ♖g2+ 76 ♔h1 ♖h2+ 77 ♔xh2**.

Black used both the prospect of stalemate and of perpetual check to save a lost endgame.

It is rare to see both used in a middlegame. But it happens:

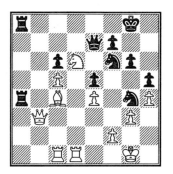

Beliavsky – Christiansen
Reggio Emilia 1987-88

Black to play

White threatens a capture on f7 but he has a harder-to-meet threat of ♕b6 and ♕xb7. After 29...♘h6 30 ♕b6 he would be winning.

Black could have set a trap with 29...♔g7 and 30 ♗xf7? ♘xe4! or 30 ♘xf7? ♘xe4. But that doesn't stop 30 ♕b6!.

Instead, he found **29...♘xf2! 30 ♔xf2 ♖a3**.

Now 31 ♕b6, the move White wanted to make, invites 31...♘g4+.

White can quickly get into trouble (32 ♔g1?? ♖xg3+ or 32 ♔g2 ♘e3+ and wins, or 32 ♔e1 ♕f6).

Safest is 32 ♔e2. But 32...♖xg3 can yield any of three results.

So White chose **31 ♗xf7+ ♔g7 32 ♕e6**.

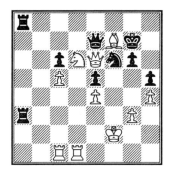

Black to play

Now what? The endgame is lost after 32...♘g4+ 33 ♔e2 ♕xe6 34 ♗xe6.

White must have thought that **32...♖a2+~** was the familiar "spite check" that a player makes before resigning.

He probably *would* have resigned after 33 ♔f1!.

Or he would eventually have resigned after 33 ♕xa2! ♖xa2+ 34 ♗xa2. White gets too much material for his queen.

He played **33 &g1** and was surprised by **33...&8a3!**.

If he captures the queen, 34...&xg3+ is the first of perpetual rook checks on the White's third rank.

Once again White could win with 34 &xa2! &xa2 35 &xa2. But that would drag the game out. Surely there is something faster, isn't there?

White to play

Well, 34 &h3! would also have won because it protects g3. But that's not the kind of move humans consider for very long.

What did fit the demands of the position was **34 &e8+!**.

Then 34...&xe8 allows 35 &xg6+ and 36 &g8 mate.

If 34...&xe8 White can just take the queen, 35 &xe8, because his queen watches the checking square h3 after 35...&xg3+ 36 &h1.

That leaves king moves. But 34...&f8 35 &xe7+ and 36 &xa2 is over. And 34...&h8 35 &xf6 &xg3+ 36 &h1 is too.

White's advantage has ballooned since 29...&xf2 and grew further after **34...&h6! 35 &xf6 &xg3+ 36 &h1**.

Black to play

But Black was not done, with **36...&xf7!** he cut his material deficit and invited 37 &xf7 &h3+ with perpetual rook checks.

Yet White had three ways to win. The most forcing was 37 &g4+!.

The point is that now when he plays ♕xf7 his queen will control a key checking square – 37...fxg4 38 ♕xf7 ♖h3+ 39 ♔g1 ♖g3+ 40 ♔f1 ♖f3+ 41 ♕xf3.

A second win was 37 ♕xe5! so that the queen controls g3, e.g. 37...♖h3+ 38 ♔g1 (38...♖f3 39 ♕g5+ ♔g7 40 ♖d7!).

But White was caught up in the tactical spirit of the position and picked the third winning move, his own queen sacrifice – **37 ♖d7!**.

Black to play

Now 37...♕xe6 38 ♖h7 mate would be the just finish. But justice failed because Black replied **37...♕xf6!** and White fell for **38 ♕xf6?? ♖h2+!**.

White must allow stalemate 39 ♔xh2 ♖g2+! 40 ♔h3 ♖g3+ or 40 ♔h1 ♖g1+.

What White missed was **38 ♖h7+!**. That releases the stalemate, so that 38...♔xh7 39 ♕xf6 wins (39...♖h3+ 40 ♔g1 ♖g3+ 41 ♔f1!).

Quiz

25.

Osmanagic – Gligoric
Sarajevo 1963

White to play

Some computers recommend 29 ♕d2. What is better?

26.

Kasparov – McDonald
Uppingham 1986

White to play

"Almost anything wins."

(a) Does that include **54 ♗xe4** ?

(b) What about 54 ♕e6+ ♔h5 55 ♗xe4 ?

27.

Shirov – Morozevich
Astana 2001

Black to play

Black rejected 55...♖xh5 56 ♖a5+ and lost after **55...♔b4 56 ♖b6+ ♔c5 57 ♖xh6**.

What did he miss?

Chapter Eleven:
The Very Lucky

"The strong are lucky," the Russian chess editor Alexander Roshal said. "The very strong are very lucky."

At the club level there are always players who regularly escape bad or lost positions, with a draw or a win. At the grandmaster level there have been players whose "luck" astonished their rivals. Among the greatest swindlers are Judith Polgar, Emanuel Lasker and Magnus Carlsen.

Polgar had her rivals shaking their heads at an international tournament in 1999 when she won three games from lost positions, against world-class opponents. But she had demonstrated her ability to nurture good fortune much earlier.

J. Polgar – Short
New York 1994

1 e4 e6 2 d4 d5 3 ♘c3 ♘f6 4 e5 ♘fd7 5 ♘ce2 c5 6 c3 ♘c6 7 f4 cxd4 8 cxd4 f5 9 ♘f3 ♘b6 10 h3 ♗e7 11 g4? ♗h4+ 12 ♘xh4? ♛xh4+ 13 ♔d2 ♛f2! 14 b3 ♘xd4

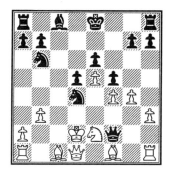

White to play

Nigel Short, who had played a world championship match one year before, is on the cusp of a blowout win. After 15 ♗b2 he could safely grab a second pawn with 15...♘xe2 and ...♛xf4+.

Or he can choose 15...♘f3+ 16 ♔c2 0-0 followed by ...♗d7/...♖ac8+, among other plans. Then he could keep the initiative and an extra pawn.

Polgar needed to find a way to dissuade him from making simple, solid moves. She found **15 ♔c3~**.

This seems to cry out for punishment. Why would such a strong player make it? Perhaps she was having a bad day. After all, she had played 11 g4? and 12 ♘xh4?, didn't she?

Rather than 15...♘f3 and 16...d4+/...♘d5, Black jumped at **15...♕f3+ 16 ♔b2! ♕xh1**.

But after **17 ♘xd4** chances were nearly equal, despite the material imbalance.

Black to play

The reason is that White's pieces, all but the knight undeveloped, have better futures than Black's pieces. This became clearer after **17...♕h2+ 18 ♔b1 0-0 19 a4 a5? 20 ♖a2! ♕g3**.

White has a number of favorable options from now on, including 21 gxf5 exf4 22 e6. That would keep Black's minor pieces out of play and prepare an attack on g7 with ♖g2 and ♗b2.

Something similar happened: **21 ♖g2 ♕c3 22 gxf5 exf5 23 ♗b2**. For example, 23...♕e3 24 ♗d3 ♗d7? 25 e6 ♗e8 26 ♖xg7+ ♔xg7 27 ♘xf5+. Or 24...g6 25 e6 and ♗xf5.

Black was lost after **23...♕c7 24 e6!**.

Black to play

The rest was **24...♖f6 25 ♘xf5 ♖g6 26.♗e5 ♕d8 27 ♘xg7 d4 28 f5 ♖xg2 29 ♗xg2 ♕g5 30 ♕h5 ♕xh5 31 ♘xh5 ♖a6 32 ♗xd4 ♘a8 33 ♗d5 resigns**.

What great swindlers have in common is tactical alertness and the emotional ability to deal with sharp changes in the position. They can "reset" themselves after they blunder. They know it is only the last mistake that counts.

Guerrero – J. Polgar
Tromso 2014

Black to play

White has sacrificed a piece but stands worse. His last move, 27 h3, can be safely ignored in view of 28 hxg4 hxg4+, when Black wins.

Instead of 27...d6, threatening ...♘xf3, Black chose **27...♖hg8?**. It has a greater threat, 28...♖xg2 (29 ♕xg2 ♖xg2 30 ♔xg2 ♕b8 followed by ...♕xb2 or ...♕g8+/...♕xd5).

She realized her error after **28 d6!** opened the diagonal leading to her king. She would lose after 30...♕b6 31 ♕e4+ ♔a7 33 ♖b3, for instance.

Computer-best is 28...♕xd6. But 29 hxg4 hxg4 30 ♕e4+! would force 30...♕c6 and a bad endgame for Black.

Polgar gambled with **28...♕c6 29 hxg4**. Computers want Black to play a lost endgame, 29...♘xf3 30 ♕xf3 ♕xf3 31 gxf3 hxg4.

But her only realistic chance lay in **29...hxg4~**.

White to play

White found **30 ♖c3!**. Then came **30...♖h8+ 31 ♔h2**.

Instead of the defeatist 31...g3? 32 ♖xg3 ♗xd6 that computers look at, Black chose **31...♕xd6~**.

She threatened 32...♖xh2+! 33 ♔xh2 ♘f3+ and mates. But **32 ♕e4+!** should have ended matters.

After **32...♘c6** there was only one good White move but it would have been crushing – 33 ♖h3! so that 33...gxh3 34 ♗xd6!. Also lost is 33...♖xh3 34 gxh3 g3 35 ♗g1.

However, White played **33 g3??**. Both players thought this would win – until Black spotted **33...♖xh2+! 34 ♔xh2 ♕d2+.**

White **resigned** in view of 35 ...♕h6+ after 35 ♔g2 or 35 ♔h1.

This was a real gamble because the endgame that would arise after 28...♕xd6 29 hxg4 hxg4 30 ♕e4+! ♕c6 31 ♕xc6+ ♘xc6 is not hopeless.

There are problems for White to solve after 32 ♖d3 ♖h8+ 33 ♗h2 ♗f2 because of the threat of ...g3. For example, 34 g3? ♘e5 or 34 ♖aa3 ♘e5.

Lucky as Usual

After another international tournament, a grandmaster rival, Alexander Grischuk, said Polgar "was lucky – as usual." He knew this first-hand.

Grischuk – J. Polgar
Wijk aan Zee 2005

Black to play

Some computers recommend 33...♖b8 to protect the b4-pawn but acknowledge a big edge for White after 34 ♘c4.

Other engines say the best defense is the minimizing 33...♖c8 34 ♘c4 ♖xc4 and then 35 ♕xc4 b3 36 ♕xb3 ♗xd6. But with only a pawn for a piece, Black is losing.

Black chose **33...♕b5~**. It holds out chances of making the position messy (34 ♗b6 b3 35 d7 ♗e7 36 ♘c3 b2!).

There was also a trick that looked scarier than it really is. On 34 ♘c4! Black has 34...♗b2!.

That looks dangerous in view of 35 ♘xb2 ♕xa5 when she has counterplay, 37 d7 ♖d8 38 ♘c5 b3! 39 ♘xb3? ♕e1+.

If White could study the position at length, he would have seen that 35 ♕xb2 ♕xc4 36 ♕xb4 should win.

Even better is the simple retreat, 35 ♕d3!, followed by pushing the d-pawn, (35...f5 36 d7 fxe4 37 d8(♕)+).

White chose **34 ♕d5**, since a trade of queens seemed to end matters (34...♕xd5 35 ♘xd5 b3 36 d7 b2 37 ♘d2).

Black replied **34...♖a7!**.

White to play

She was waiting for 35 ♘c5 b3!. Black wins after 36 ♕xb3? ♗xc5 and draws after 36 ♘xb3 ♕xd5 37 ♘xd5 ♗xd6. She would have the edge after 36 d7 ♖xd7 37 ♘xd7 b2.

That b-pawn almost equalizes chances in variations such as 35 ♗c7 b3! 36 d7 ♗e7 37 d8(♕)+ ♗xd8 38 ♕xd8+ ♔h7 and ...b2.

Instead, White traded queens, **35 ♕xb5 axb5**. In the back of the minds of both players is the prospect of an endgame in which White has two pieces against a rook.

Can he win after, say, 36 ♗c7 b3 37 ♘c3 b2 38 ♘ed5 ♗xd6! 39 ♗xd6 ♖a1+ 40 ♔f2 ♖d1? No.

So he chose **36 ♗b6 ♖d7 37 ♗c5!** to stop the b-pawn at least temporarily.

Black was virtually forced into **37...♗c1 38 ♘d5 b3**.

White to play

The b-pawn was Black's only source of counterplay. It turns out to be enough:

After 39 ♘ef6+ gxf6 40 ♘xf6+ ♔g7! 41 ♘xd7 she can stop ♗e5+ with 41...f6!.

White is not winning after 42 ♘xf6 ♗e3+! – and is losing after 42 ♗d4? ♗e3+! (43 ♗xe3 b2).

Another drawing line is 42 ♘f8 b2 43 ♘e6+ ♔g6 44 d7.

White might still have won after 39 ♔f2 b2 40 ♘ec3. For example, 40...♗d2 41 ♘b1 ♗a5 42 ♔e3.

But he went with **39 ♗b4 b2 40 ♘ec3** and after **40...♗d2! 41 ♔f2 b1(♕) 42 ♘xb1 ♗xb4 43 ♘xb4 ♖xd6** his winning chances had disappeared. He agreed to a draw after **44 ♔e3**.

After the tournament, Grischuk conceded that Polgar's continual good fortune was no accident. "The fact that a person has been lucky for so many years means something more," he said.

Lucky Lasker

Long before Polgar stole points and half points from grandmasters, Emanuel Lasker was angering rivals with his seemingly unending luck. After Lasker won one of the first great international tournaments, Nuremberg 1896, his rival Siegbert Tarrasch retaliated. He wrote a tournament book with the usual crosstable but also with a "luck" table.

This purported to show how Lasker got five underserved points by winning from five lost positions. Without those lucky points, Lasker would have finished in the middle of the 19-player field, Tarrasch suggested.

How lucky was Lasker? Let's see.

Lasker – Schallopp
Nuremberg 1896

1 d4 d5 2 ♘f3 ♘f6 3 c4 e6 4 ♘c3 ♗e7 5 ♗f4 0-0 6 c5 b6 7 b4 a5 8 a3 ♘e4! 9 ♘xe4? dxe4 10 ♘e5 f6 11 ♘c4 axb4 12 axb4 ♖xa1 13 ♕xa1 ♘c6 14 ♕c3 ♘xd4 (14...♘xb4! 15 ♕xb4 ♕xd4 is also strong) **15 e3 ♘f5**

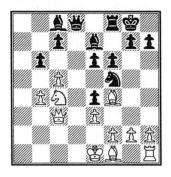

White to play

Black is ready to win a second pawn with 16...bxc5.

Some computers recommend 16 cxb6 cxb6. But the open c-file benefits Black. For example, 17 ♗e2 e5 18 ♗g3 ♕c7! carries a threat of ...b5. Black would be making progress after 19 ♕b2 ♗e6 20 ♘d2 ♖a8 or 20...♖c8.

Other computers surrender a white pawn with 16 h3 or 16 ♗e2 and search for drawable endgames.

Lasker opted for **16 ♘d2~**. It (a) allows the queen to protect the c5-pawn, (b) attacks the Black e4-pawn and (c) frees c4 for White's f1-bishop.

And taken together we can add: (d) It gives White chances for more than a grueling defense.

Nevertheless, Black has a big advantage, which could have grown after 16...bxc5 17 bxc5 and now 17...e5 18 ♗g3 h5 or 17...g5 18 ♗g3 h5.

Black preferred **16...♗b7**, so that he can continue 17 ♗c4 ♗d5 and ...♕d7/...♖a8.

He had calculated a temporary piece sacrifice: **17 c6** was answered by **17...♗xc6 18 ♕xc6 ♗xb4**.

Black would win back a piece and keep the initiative after 19 ♕xe6+ ♔h8 20 ♕a2 g5 21 ♗g3 ♕e7 and ...♖d8.

Lasker chose **19 ♕c2!**.

Black to play

Things look bleak. After 19...♕d7 Black would threaten to win the pinned knight with 20...♖d8 or bring the rook to good use after 20...♖a8 and ...♖a1+.

But Lasker intended 20 ♗c4 so that 20...♖d8 21 0-0 followed by ♕xe4 would allow him to escape into a middlegame with only a slight disadvantage.

Black can improve on this, such as with 20...b5 or 20...♔h8 and 21...e5. But his superiority would remain slight. His 16...♗b7? had hurt him.

Black chose **19...♕d5** because it seemed to discourage 20 ♗c4 ♗xd2+ 21 ♕xd2 ♕xc4. He was wrong: **20 ♗c4! ♗xd2+ 21 ♔e2** left his queen and d2-bishop hanging.

217

The best he could get was **21...♛c6 22 ♔xd2 ♖d8+ 23 ♔e2** but his initiative was over and his three extra pawns didn't compensate for the lost bishop.

As often happened, a Lasker opponent couldn't deal with the swift change in fortune. Black compounded his miscalculation with **23...♖d5? 24 ♛b3! ♖c5 25 ♗xe6+ ♔f8**.

White did not fall for 26 ♗xf5 ♖c2+ 27 ♔e1 ♖c1+ but played **26 ♖d1** and won easily.

What Lasker showed, when he played 16 ♘d2 and in some of his other great swindles, was that he preferred moves that offered a fighting chance – ideally a winning chance, even when they were not objectively best.

Magnus the Swindler

Vladimir Kramnik paid the ultimate compliment to Magnus Carlsen. Looking at the position on the Norwegian's board, Kramnik said, "It's completely equal – which means Magnus will win."

It is not just equal positions that he wins. He had such a lost position against Hikaru Nakamura in one of their games (Zurich 2014) that computers rated Nakamura's advantage at +10.00. That is more than an extra queen. Of course, Carlsen won.

He was already an accomplished swindler at age 12.

Carlsen – Olszewski
Budva 2003

White to play

Carlsen had been lost for more than 20 moves and his disadvantage steadily grew until it reached more than -10.00. If he had played 50 ♘b5 Black could choose between making a second queen or mating with 50...♛d1+ and 51...♛f1!.

Carlsen didn't resign. But his **50 ♛d8** was little more than a bluff.

There is no perpetual check after 50...♛xc3! because 51 ♛g5+ ♔h7 52 ♛h5+ ♔g8 53 ♛g5+ can be met by 53...♘g7.

Even the cautious 50...♘e7 wins (51 ♛a5 a2 52 ♘xa2 ♛d1+ 53 ♔h2 ♛f1).

But Black made what looked like another safety-move, **50...♖e7??**.

He realized what he had done after **51 ♘e3!** made the black knight and rook vulnerable.

Black to play

Now 51...♕xc3 is only a draw in view of 52 ♘xf5+ ♔f6 53 ♕xe7+! ♔xf5 54 ♕h7+! with perpetual check.

The other capture, 51...♘xe3 52 ♕xe7+, leads to another draw after 52...♔h8! (not 52...♔g8 53 ♕g5+ and ♕xe3).

Black can't do more than draw after 51...♖f7 52 ♕g5+ ♔h8 53 ♘xf5.

He played the best practical move, **51...♔g6!**. It was best simply because it made finding the right path to a draw harder.

White to play

It was harder because 52 ♕g8+ offers a White a chance to win, 52...♖g7?? 53 ♕e6+ ♔h7 54 ♕xf5+ ♔g8 55 ♘e4.

But after 52...♘g7 White would have to find the one saving sequence – 53 ♘f5! ♔xf5 54 ♕h7+! ♔f6 55 ♘e4+.

Then 55...♔f7?? 56 ♘xd6 mates. So the game would end with 55...♕xe4! 56 ♕xe4 ♖a7! and White has to go for perpetual check before the a-pawn queens.

Instead, Carlsen went for the direct **52 ♘xf5**. If Black could bring himself to the realization that his win was gone, he would have played 52...♔xf5 53 ♕xe7 ♕xc3 and allowed perpetual check.

He wasn't ready for a handshake yet and played **52...♕xc3 53 ♘xe7+ ♔f7**.

White to play

The a-pawn and the threat of ...♕e1+ seemed decisive. But **54 ♔h2!** saved White.

What is more, if Black wanted a draw he would have to search for one. (The right way is 54...♕e1!, so that 55 h4! ♕f1 forces White to give perpetual check with 56 ♕g8+! ♔xe7 57 ♕e6+.)

Instead, Black chose **54...♕b2?? 55 h4! ♕xf2+ 56 ♔h3 ♕g2+** and discovered he was losing after **57 ♔g4 f2 58 ♕d7!**. He was mated seven moves later.

Like Lasker, Carlsen developed an instinct for defensive moves that contained at least the hint of aggression. He tried to deny opponents the transition to an endgame with a big advantage. It was better to grab the chance to turn the game around.

Gagunashvili – Carlsen
Wijk aan Zee 2004

Black to play

Black would have slim chances in an endgame, after 28...♕e3 or 28...♕e7, as recommended by some computers. Or after 28...♕d8 29 ♘c4 ♕e7 30 ♕d6, as cited by others.

The Carlsen choice was **28...♕f6~**. It requires White to make a major decision.

Should he try to force an endgame with 29 ♕d6 ? Once he examines that move, White would notice that it threatens to win outright with 30 ♗d1! and ♗a4+.

That convinced White to consider an alternative 29th move.

White to play

The immediate **29 ♗d1** threatened 30 ♗a4+ ♚d8 31 ♕d6+ ♚c8 32 ♗d7+ and wins.

White must have been disappointed to see, after **29...♘e7**, that 30 ♗a4+ ♚f8 is nothing.

It's worse than that because Black threatened to get the upper hand with 31...♖xh6.

He would not fear 31 ♕e3 ♘f5! 32 ♕c5+ ♕e7 because that pawn is falling, 33 ♕xe7+ ♚xe7 34 g4 ♖xh6!.

White decided that if he was going to trade queens, the right way was **30 ♕f3**.

Black to play

He was right about 30...♕xf3 31 gxf3. Computers recommend it but White would be winning after 31...♘f5 32 h7, for example.

Carlsen again avoided a queen trade, **30...♘f5~**.

That is very risky since 31 ♘g4 would win fairly easily after 31...♛d4 32 ♖xf5.

More calculation is required by 31...♛e7 since 32 ♖xf5? ♗xf5 is a check. (With enough time, it becomes easier to see that 32 ♛c3! would win.)

Giving a check in time pressure is natural, so **31 ♗a4+ ♚f8**.

By putting his pieces on active squares (28...♛f6~ and 30...♘f5~) Black threatened to balance chances by winning the h6-pawn. He would be at least equal after 32 ♘g4 ♛a1+ 33 ♗d1 ♛xa5+.

White to play

As an apprentice swindler, Carlsen was also learning how to recognize when the tide was turning in his favor.

On **32 ♛a3+** there was no reason for 32...♛e7, even though computers say 33 ♛xe7+ ♚xe7 is about equal. Black can begin thinking about winning.

With **32...♚g8!** he made possible that third result (33...♛xe5+).

White's last move ruled out ...♛a1+ and prepared **33 ♘g4!**.

After **33...♛d4!** the g4-knight was hanging and 34...♛g1+ was also in the air.

White to play

The change in fortune was evident in the difficulty White had in trying to navigate towards a draw. It would have taken calm nerves to calculate 34 ♛f3! ♛xa4 35 ♖xf5!.

Then 35...♕a1+ 36 ♔f2 ♕b2+ 37 ♔g1 ♗xf5 38 ♕xf5 ♕c1+ and 39...♖xh6(+)! draws.

White played the most natural move, **34 ♗d1**. Then 34...♕g1+ 35 ♔d2 ♕xg2+? 36 ♗e2 when the crisis is over, or 35...♔h7 36 ♕d3!.

Once again, it made sense to avoid forcing moves when an opponent is short of time. That meant **34...♔h7!**.

After the game it became evident that White was lost because Black's rook can enter play at d8 (35...♕g1+ 36 ♔d2 ♖d8+) or at c8 (35 ♗e2 ♖c8!) or even e8 (35 ♘f2 ♗c4! and ...♖e8+). White resigned after a few mutual errors. Another two-step swindle (31 ♗a4+?? and 34 ♗d1??)

Such Fantastic Luck

After Carlsen started beating world-class opponents, they complained about his luck. Veselin Topalov blundered to him at Wijk aan Zee 2008 and said the young Norwegian would be harmed by expecting his good fortune to continue:

"I don't think this is good for Magnus, such fantastic luck. You know he should have lost three games but he won all three!"

Carlsen – Topalov
Morelia-Linares 2008

White to play

A pawn up, Black would be on the road to victory after 23 ♖aa1 ♘c4 (and more so after 23 ♖b4? ♕d6 traps the rook).

White chose **23 ♖d4~**. To accept the Exchange sacrifice means conceding control of key dark squares, such as 23...♗xd4 24 ♗xd4 (threat of ♕f6) ♕d6 25 ♗f6 ♖fe8 26 e5 and ♘e4.

But Black can improve with 24...f5!. Then White is not close to compensation for his sacrificed material. For instance, 25 exf5 ♕d8! 26 ♕f2 ♖xf5 27 ♗g4 ♖f7.

Black didn't trust that and chose **23...♖ad8**. Play went **24 e5 ♖xd4 25 ♗xd4 c5 26 ♗e3**.

Black to play

With only an extra pawn, Black had to be careful. Trading bishops, 26...♗c4, would lose that pawn, 27 ♗xc4 ♘xc4 28 ♘d5, and extinguish most of his advantage.

That is why safeguarding the pawn, 26...b6!, made sense.

But so did trying to liquidate the powerful e5-pawn with **26...f6**.

Then came **27 ♘b5 ♕d8** (based on 28 ♗xc5 fxe5! and 29 ♗e7 ♕b6+ 30 ♔h1 ♖f5! with good winning chances).

Computers like 28 e6 but Magnus played **28 f5**.

After **28...dxe5** spectators – and some fellow grandmasters – thought his idea was to try to hold the endgame after 29 ♕g4 ♕b6! 30 fxg6 ♕xg6 31 ♕xg6 and ♗xc5.

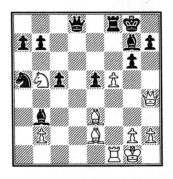

White to play

But his idea was actually to play to win with **29 ♗g5~** and 30 f6.

Black cannot afford 29...♗f6?? 30 fxg6!.

But 29...♕d7 30 f6 a6! was a good reply, in view of 31 ♘c3 ♕d4+! or 31 fxg7 ♖xf1+ 32 ♗xf1 axb5.

It seemed just as good to play **29...♕b6** because Black threatened 30...c4+ and 31...♕xb5.

There was no turning back (30 ♔h1 ♖xf5).

So play went **30 f6! c4+ 31 ♔h1 ♕xb5 32 fxg7 ♖xf1+ 33 ♗xf1 ♔xg7**.

224

White to play

An attacking player naturally feels that the dark squares can be exploited in a position like this. But 34 ♗h6+ ♔f7 35 ♕d8 is only mildly dangerous (35...♗c2 36 ♕h8 ♗d3 37 ♕xh7+ ♔e6).

White set a trap with **34 ♗d8**. His main threat was 35 ♕e7+ ♔g8 38 ♕e6+ ♔f8 39 ♗e7+.

Black covered e7 with **34...♘c6??** and resigned after **35 ♕f6+ ♔g8 36 ♕e6+ ♔f8 37 ♗g5!**.

Black had to allow perpetual check, e.g. 34...♕d5 35 ♕e7+ ♔g8 36 ♕e8+ ♔g7.

Hard Work

Carlsen's success was far from accidental. "Carlsen often saves bad positions or wins drawish positions because he keeps playing and trying to push and make the most of the result," said Fabiano Caruana. "From the outside it might look like luck, but it's really more the result of hard work."

Rather it is hard work and practicing good swindle skills, such as identifying the best tactical resource:

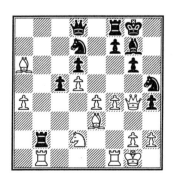

Ponomariev – Carlsen
Bazna 2010

Black to play

225

After the expected exchange 21...♖xb1 22 ♖xb1 White would be ready to prepare the decisive advance of his a-pawn, with 23 ♗b5 ♘b6 24 ♗c6 and 25 a5.

Black can avert this with 22...♕a5! so that 23 ♕xd7 ♕xa6 24 ♕b5 ♖a8.

But with two bishops and an outside passed pawn White should win after 23 ♗b5!, e.g. 23...♘b6 24 ♕xh4 or 23...♗d4 24 ♗xd4 ♕xd2 25 ♗f2.

The only other option in the diagram seemed to be 21...♖a2. But Carlsen apparently didn't like the looks of 22 ♗b5.

He found a third option, **21...♖xd2~** and **22 ♗xd2 ♗d4+**.

White to play

His trainer, Peter-Heine Nielsen, conceded, that his 21st move was "objectively a losing sacrifice." But it gives Black tactical chances, whereas "other moves simply leave Black a pawn down in a worse position."

Carlsen recognized a mating pattern: If White's king is driven to h1, Black can try to open the h-file with ...♘g3+ and then hxg3/...hxg3. Black delivers a fatal check on the h-file with his queen or rook.

This sounds more fantasy than real. So let's analyze 23 ♔h1 and the move Carlsen intended, 23...♘df6.

Then 24 ♕xh4 ♘xe4 sets the stage for that pattern: 25 ♕xd8 ♖xd8 26 ♗e1?? does not stop 26...♘hg3+! 27 ♗xg3? ♘xg3+ 28 hxg3 ♔g7! and ...♖h8 mates. (Or 27 hxg3 ♔g7 28 ♗f2 ♘xf2+ and wins.)

White can give back the Exchange with the immediate 25 ♗e1! and try to win the pawn-up ending after 25...♕xh4 26 ♗xh4 ♘d2.

Does White have anything clearer than that?

Well, White can try 24 ♕f3, rather than 24 ♕xh4.

23 ♔h1 ♘df6 24 ♕f3

Black to play

Then the mating idea, 24...♘g3+ 25 hxg3 hxg3, threatens to win with 26...♔g7!.

There is only one good reply, 26 ♗e1!. Black can play 26...♘xe4! (threat of 27...♕h4 mate) and 27 ♗xg3 ♘xg3+ 28 ♕xg3 ♔g7.

But in this version, White emerges with an extra piece after an "only" move, 29 ♖f2!.

Finally, there is a third White option, 24 ♕h3! instead of 24 ♕xh4 and 24 ♕f3.

A key difference is that 24...♘xe4 25 ♗e1 ♘hg3+ (25...♕a8!) 26 hxg3 hxg3 now fails to 27 ♗d3 ♔g7 28 ♗xe4 and White's mountain of material prevails after 28...♖h8 29 ♗xg3 ♖xh3+ 30 gxh3.

But with his clock ticking White failed to find these wins and chose **23 ♖f2?**. There followed **23...♗xf2+ 24 ♔xf2 ♘df6**.

White to play

Compared with the diagram on page 225, it seems that all that has happened is a trade of rooks and minor pieces. But Black's remaining pieces are more active than White's.

That means something after 25 ♕e2 ♖e8 26 ♗d3 ♘xe4+ 27 ♗xe4 ♘f6 and he gets the pawn back with the better chances.

In the game, **25 ♕f3 ♕e8!** also won a pawn and eventually the game after **26 e5 ♕xa4 27 exf6 ♕xa6.**

So, yes, 21...♖xd2 should have lost a bad position faster. But it gave Black a chance to make himself lucky.

Justified Dice Throw

Before Carlsen became world champion, many of his swindles were the result of gambles like that. Here is a more justified throw of the dice.

Motylev – Carlsen
Biel 2007

Black to play

Black doesn't want to allow fxg6 but can't play 32...gxf5 in view of 33 ♘xf5.

For example, 33...♖g8 34 ♖f1 ♘e8 and now 35 ♘xg7 ♘xg7? 36 ♕xg8+! ♔xg8 37 ♖f8 mate.

Black might try 32...♖d8 so that 33 fxg6 ♖d7! 34 ♗e7 hxg6 complicates.

But 33 ♖a1 and ♖a7 (or ♗a5!) should win. For example, 33...♕c6 34 ♖a7 ♖d7 35 ♖xd7 ♕xd7 36 fxg6.

Carlsen identified his best tactical resource with **32...e4**. He can try to exploit the diagonal leading to the white king after ...♕b8.

For instance, 33 ♖xe4 ♖xe4 (not 33...♘xe4 34 ♕xe8+) 34 ♘xe4 looks promising in view of 34...gxf5?? 35 ♘xf6 and wins.

But Black can improve with 34...♕b8+! (35 ♘d6 ♘e4 and 35 ♗d6 ♕e8!).

There was a lot more to calculate, including 33 ♖xe4 ♖xe4 34 ♗f8! ♗xf8 35 ♕xf8+ ♘g8 36 ♘xe4.

But White naturally kept his kingside tactics alive with **33 fxg6** and Black replied **33...♕b8!**.

White to play

Black's chances on the diagonal begin to surface after 34...♘h5 or 34...♖d8 followed by ...♖d3!. There is also the prospect of pushing the e-pawn (34...e3, 35...e2 and 36...♖e3).

White was short on time but long on choices. He still had the idea of ♖a1-a7, for instance.

He could calculate 34 ♖a1 ♘h5 and see that 35 ♗d6! ♕xd6 36 ♕xe8+ wins immediately. (Remember that ♗d6 move.)

There was also 34 ♖f1!, threatening ♖xf6. Again 34...♘h5 fails to 35 ♗d6!.

The game would also end after 34...♕e5 35 ♖xf6! in view of 35...♗xf6 36 ♕xh7 mate and 35...♕xf6 36 ♕xe8+.

Nevertheless, White began to miss tactics. He played **34 gxh7**. It pockets another pawn and ruled out 34...♘h5.

Black to play

Black could have tried 34...♖d8 with a winning threat of 35...♖d3!.

After 35 ♕g6 ♖d3 White must avoid 36 ...♖xg3! 37 ♕xg3 ♘g4+! 38 hxg4 ♗e5 and Black wins.

Unfortunately for him, White can defend with 36 ♖f1. Then at the end of the 36...♖xg3 combination he can get the queen back with 39 ♖f8+.

That might have been a better try than **34...♕e5** because his only real threat is 35...♗h6 and 36...♗f4.

229

Even if White allowed 35...♗h6 he could win with 36 ♖f1 ♗f4 37 ♔h1! and then 37...♗xg3 38 ♖xf6 e3 39 ♖g6 mates.

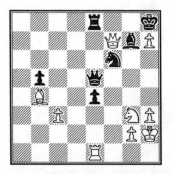

White to play

But White was perplexed by his choices, including 35 ♖f1 and 35 ♕g6. In fact, when White played 34 gxh7 he had planned on the game going 34...♕e5 35 ♕g6. That should win after 35...e3 36 ♔g1 and ♘f5/♗d6. Or 35...♖d8 36 ♖f1 ♖d3 37 ♗f8!.

But when the position occurred on the board he saw a way to force a very favorable, if not won endgame – 35 ♗d6 (the key move in variations we considered earlier) ♕xd6 36 ♕xg7+ ♔xg7 37 ♘f5+ ♔xh7 38 ♘xd6.

Unfortunately, after **35 ♗xd6??** **♕xd6** he suddenly realized that his knight is still pinned – and 37 ♘f5+ would be illegal. He **resigned**.

Magnus the Confuser

And when all else failed, Carlsen confused his opponents.

Viktor Korchnoi watched in stunned silence as the following game reached its final stage. White had three minutes and his opponent had nine seconds – and a lost position. When it ended, Korchnoi threw up his hands and exclaimed to a grandmaster colleague, Gennady Sosonko, "Did you see that? Nine seconds! Incredible."

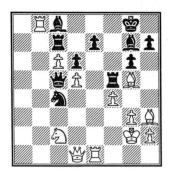

Van Wely – Carlsen
Wijk aan Zee 2008

Black to play

How lost is Black? Let us count the ways:

His c7-rook and c8-bishop are paralyzed. He must lose at least the e7-pawn. Any endgame is lost because of White's protected passed c6-pawn.

The computer-best 30...♖f8, allows White to trade twice on c8 and reach a stable, easier to understand position that engines rate as a White advantage of more than +2.

Black went for **30...♘b2~** and that advantage nearly ballooned.

Spectators saw **31 ♕f3! ♕xc2+~ 32 ♖e2.**

Black to play

Carlsen must have been preparing 32...♘d3, some thought. Then 33 ♖xc2 ♘e1+ 34 ♔f2 ♘xf3 gets the queen back.

But surely that is lost after 35 ♗xf5 gxf5 36 ♔xf3.

It is, so Black quickly replied **32...♕b1 33 ♗xf5 ♕xf5.**

He is "loster" and seemed to be playing moves out of sheer inertia. But he now had some tactical ideas, such as 34...♕h3+. If he could play 34...♔f7 he would be poised for 35...♕h3+ 36 ♔h1 ♗g4! – and Black is winning (37 ♕g2 ♕h5).

White stopped that with **34 g4! ♕f7.**

White to play

Black's rook and c8-bishop remain immobile and his knight is virtually offsides at b2. But he has one strange asset: White's position is so overwhelming he doesn't know when to stop taking more material.

Should he swap rooks with 35 ♖xe7 ? Or take on e7 with the bishop so that ♗xd6 is coming ?

If he wants to assure himself of a technical win, White's best is 35 ♖xe7 ♖xe7 36 ♗xe7 and then 36...♕xe7 37 ♖xc8+ or 36...♕e8 37 ♕e4.

Computers prefer **35 ♗xe7** so that 35...♘c4 36 ♕e4.

Black's **35...h5!** kept fleeting hopes alive, even if they live only in fantasy variations such as 36 gxh5 ♔h7 37 hxg6+ ♕xg6+ 38 ♕g3 ♗g4 39 ♖exb2?? ♕e4+ 40 ♔g1 ♗d4+ with a draw.

White to play

White ignored it and play went **36 ♗xd6! hxg4**.

He evaded what seemed like the last trap (37 ♕xg4? ♕xd5+) with **37 ♕e4**.

White added a new threat of ♕e8+ to that of 38 ♗xc7 and 38 ♖exb2.

From Black's point of view, the greatest threat was a trade of queens. That would eliminate his last chances for perpetual check or double attacks by the queen.

He played **37...♔h7!**, simply so ♕e8 is not check.

White to play

With three moves to go before the time control, White could have played 38 ♖bxb2 and wait for Black to resign after 38...♗f5 39 ♕c4 ♗xb2 40 ♗xc7.

Instead, he played the also-winning **38 ♗xc7** and had to find an answer to **38...♗f5**.

That was a problem because the chief tactic lurking in the position for some time was the possibility of ...♕xd5+. Where does the White king go then?

That is very difficult to calculate in your own time pressure. After the game it seemed simple: 39 ♕e7! ♕xd5+ 40 ♔g1!.

Then there is no perpetual check after 40...♕d4+ 41 ♔f1 ♕d1+ 42 ♔f2. Computers call that a more than +8 advantage, nearly an extra queen.

However, White played the safer-looking **39 ♕e3?? ♕xd5+**.

White to play

Now 40 ♔g1 loses to 40...♗d4. Or does it? White didn't have time to check out the reply 41 ♖h8+! followed by 42 ♗e5(+), which keeps White on top.

Instead he played **40 ♔g3**, perhaps because he realized 40...♗d4 would lose to 41 ♗e5!.

However, **40...♘c4!** raised the luck quotient. Computers later found a bizarre way for White to continue to fight (41 ♖d8! ♕xc6 42 ♕b3 ♕xc7 43 ♖d5).

But White chose the more rational **41 ♕f2?**, a blunder worse than 40 ♔g3?. White was getting mated after **41...♕d3+ 42 ♔g2** (42 ♔h4 ♗f6 mate) **♗e4+ 43 ♖xe4 ♕xe4+ 44 ♔f1 ♕d3+ 45 ♕e2? ♘d2+**.

Korchnoi had an explanation for what he had witnessed. "Without parapsychology, that is impossible!"

No, without confusion it is impossible.

Quiz

He who lives by the swindle...

28.

Motylev – Carlsen
Wijk aan Zee 2007

Black to play

What is White's threat? How did **37...♖b4** parry it? And how did White still manage to draw?

29.

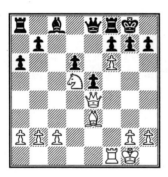

Showalter – Lasker
Kokomo 1893

Black to play

Computers recommend the minimizing move 19...g5 to avoid fxg7. They give 20 ♗xg5 ♔h8 21 ♗h6 ♖g8 22 ♗g7+ ♖xg7 23 fxg7+ ♔xg7 24 ♘c7 as best, even though it is resignable.

What is the most hopeful defense?

Quiz Answers

1. There were two reasons. First, it required Black to find a more difficult defense than would 50 ♖gxg7 ♕f1!, which threatens 51...♕f4+.

Second, it held out the hope of winning, not just of perpetual check. Black felt that the game was over after **50 ♖dxg7 ♔e8??**.

He overlooked **51 ♖a7!**. *(diagram)*

White threatens 52 ♖g8 mate, and 51...♖f2 53 ♖g8+ ♖f8 54 ♖a8+ is lost. Play went **51...♔f8** but then **52 ♖a8+ ♔f7 53 ♖ag8!** set up an unstoppable 55 ♖g7 mate. Black would have won after 50...♖f2!.

2. There were three. The first was 56...♖a1?? instead of 56...♔f2! and 57...♗e2+.

The second was 58...♖f2?? instead of 58...♔f2!. The final one was 62...♔f1?? instead of 62...♔h2.

3. 88 ♔b1?? should have lost to 90...♖xg1 as the game went. But **90...e1(♕)??** saved him. White should have drawn with 88 ♗xg1 ♖a1+ 89 ♔d2 ♖d1+ 90 ♔c3 ♖xg1 91 ♖xe2 ♔xe2 92 ♔b4.

4. 31...♗d7! forced **32 ♕xa8** because 32 ♕f7? ♘e4+! and 32 ♕h5 ♖g8! lose. After **32...e5!** *(diagram):*

Now 33 ♖hf1 ♘d3 34 h4! retains winning chances.

White was lost after **33 ♘h3?? ♕g6+ 34 ♔f2 ♘d3+ 35 ♔f1 ♘xc1.**

5. There was nothing to lose so **38...f4~** was played. It hardly mattered that 39 ♕c7+! would win quickly.

White didn't play it because he apparently saw 39...♖d7 40 ♕xc8?? ♕xd2+ and Black wins – and didn't see that 40 ♕c4+! mates (40...♔g6 41 ♖g1+ or 40...♔f8 41 ♕xc8+).

There weren't many traps to fall into because even 39 ♖d3 ♗f5 wins for White after 40 ♖b7+ ♔g6 41 ♕xg7+. Nevertheless he chose **39 ♖f3??** and almost all of this superiority had evaporated after **39...♗f5+ 40 ♔c1** since

40...♖xd2 would have reached a double-edged ending after 41 ♕xd2 ♕g1+ 42 ♕d1 ♕xd1+.

But **40...♖c8??** *(diagram)* should have lost to 41 ♖b7+ and 42 ♖c7!. Instead, it won (!) following **41 ♘c4?? ♕g1+ 42 ♔d2 ♖d8+ 43 ♔e2 ♕xb1** (44 ♖xf4 ♔g8 or 44 ♘e5+ ♔e6! 45 ♕c6+ ♔xe5).

6. 30 ♕xe4 only prolongs a lost game (30...♕xe4 31 ♘xe4 ♘xd1 32 ♗xb4 ♖e8 and ...♖e2).

White tried **30 ♘d7~**. It should have lost to 30...♕d6!. But Black played **30...♕d4??** with the same idea (31 ♖xd4 ♖f1 mate). Unfortunately, **31 ♕xh7+! ♔xh7 32 ♘xf8+** and **33 ♖xd4** won for White.

7. After **42...♖eg6!** White should repeat the position and draw, 43 ♕d5+! ♖e6 44 ♕c5!.

Tal fell into a trap, **43 ♖xc7?? ♖xg2+!**. He would be mated after 44 ♔xg2 ♗f3+. He resigned shortly after **44 ♔f1 ♕d8!**.

Note that he could have played to win with 43 ♕xf5 ♖xg2+! 44 ♔f1!. But then 44...♕e8 sets a new trap, 45 ♖xc7 ♕d8! 46 ♖c8?? ♗e2+! and Black wins. White could draw, instead, with 46 ♖d7! ♖xf2+! 47 ♔e1.

8. Black drew after **29 ♕e7 ♖xg2+! 30 ♔xg2 ♕g4+ 31 ♔f2 ♕xh4+**, e.g. 32 ♔e3 ♕d4+ 33 ♔e2 ♕xc4+.

But **28...♖d2??** should have lost to 29 ♕f4! followed by 30 ♕xd2 or 30 ♖xg6+!.

9. (a) 37...♖xb5?? 38 ♗h6+ and ♖e8 mate.

(b) No, after 37...g5! Black eliminated ♗h6+ and threatened ...♖xb5. The game was drawn after 38 ♖g6 ♖xb5 39 ♗xg5 ♖b1+ 40 ♔f2 ♖b2+. No better was 38 ♖a5 ♔f7 39 ♖h6 ♔g7.

(c) Slowly preparing to push the queenside pawns, such as beginning with 37 ♔f2, would win.

10. After 33 ♘e7 White threatens 34 ♘c8+ ♔a8 35 ♘cb6+ ♔a7 36 ♖c8! and ♖a8 mate..

There were two traps. Black would lose after 33...a5? 34 ♘c8+ ♔a6 35 a4! threatens ♘c5 mate. Or after 33...b5? 34 ♖c7+ ♘b7? 35 ♘c6+ and mates.

After **33 ♖c8! ♘c6 34 ♘5b6!** the game was agreed drawn. But Black is lost because of the ♖a8 mate threat, e.g. 34...♕g1+ 35 ♔c2 ♘d4+ 36 ♔c3 ♕c1+ 37 ♔b4 ♕xb2+ 38 ♔c5 ♕a3+ 39 ♔d5.

11. His best tactical try is **36...♕d7!** so that 37...♖xa2+! 38 ♚xa2 ♕a4+ and 39...♕xb3+, with at least perpetual check.

This would fail after 37 ♘xe6 ♕xe6 38 ♕xg3. But White didn't want to trade his knight.

He played **37 ♕d1?** and was surprised by **37...♕b5!,** with a threat of 38...♕a5!. (*diagram*)

Black would be better in the endgame after **38 ♖g2 ♖xg2 39 ♘xg2 ♕d3 40 ♕xd3 exd3.** Instead, White played **40 ♕h1?** and resigned after **40...♕c2 41 ♘f4 g2** (41...♕f2!) **42 ♘xg2? a5 43 ♘f4 a4!.**

12. It is not winning a pawn that makes 42 ♕xd5! best but the threat of 43 ♗c5.

Then Black cannot win because, for example, 42...♕b1+ 43 ♚h2 ♕f5 allows 44 ♖xf8+ and mate next.

White chose **42 ♖c8?**, which makes 42...♕b1+ and ...♕f5 a winning plan.

But he chose **42...♕e4** and resigned after **43 ♖xf8+!.** (*diagram*)

His last move deserved a question mark. But resigning deserved two. Even short of time he should have played the only legal move, 43...♚xf8. He didn't because he saw 44 ♗c5+ ♚g8 again allows a last rank mate, 45 ♕c8+.

But after 44...♖e7! White has nothing better than 45 ♗xe7+ ♚e8 46 ♕xe4 dxe4. Then the black pawns are better than the white bishop.

13. 35...♘xf4! drew after **36 hxg4 ♘e2+** and ...♘xd4. White would have won easily after 35 ♘c6! so that 36 ♘e7+ and 37 e6+.

14. Black queens the b-pawn after 34...♗e4! and 35...b4.

15. After 38 ♘f2! Black can resign because 38...♖xe3 39 ♖xe3 traps the queen.

16. 43...c5! so that 44 bxc5 ♕h1+ 45 ♚d2 ♕g2+ with perpetual check. Or 44 dxc5 ♖xb4.

White tried **44 b5** but chances were equal after his king was exposed, **44...cxd4 45 ♕c8+ ♚h7 46 ♖h2 ♕e1+ 47 ♚c2 d3+ 48 ♚b3 ♕b1+.** (*diagram*)

It was time to accept a draw, 49 ♔a3. But the game went **49 ♖b2?? ♕d1+ 50 ♔b4 ♖a7 51 ♕xe6 ♕e1+ 52 ♔a3** and **resigns**.

17. After **29 ♖e5?? ♕c1+ 30 ♔g2 ♗d3!** he had overlooked the threat of 31...♕f1 mate. He said he had to "scramble to save his skin" after **31 h4 ♗c7**. Then 32 ♖e8+ ♔h7 33 ♕xc7 allows perpetual queen checks, 33...♕f1+ 34 ♔h2 ♕xf2+ (and not 34 ♔g3 ♕g1+ 35 ♔f4 ♕h2+).

It would have been an easy win after 29 ♖e8+ ♔h7 30 ♔g2.

18. 40 ♗e4?? lost to **40...♖a3!** (41 ♖xa3 ♕xf1+ or 41 ♖ad1 ♕xa6). There was nothing wrong with 40 a7 ♖xf3 41 gxf3 because of 41...♕h4 42 ♖a2 ♕xh3+ 43 ♔g1, for example. White would also have won with 40 ♗e2!.

19. (a) Both should win but 23 ♕b3 gets queens off the board, 23...♘c2+ 24 ♔d2 and 24...♕xb3 25 axb3 ♘xa1 26 ♖xa1. White has more than enough material, e.g. 26...♔f6 27 ♘b6 and 28 ♖a7. It would have won faster than 23 ♕e2.

(b) As a practical matter, 24 ♔d2 tried to win too quickly. Good enough was 24 ♔f1 e4 and the plan of 25 ♘b6 and pushing the a-pawn.

White was still winning until 27 ♖xf8? but by then the best moves were hard to find, such as 27 ♘c7 (27...♕xc7? 28 ♕xe4).

Computers tell us 30 b3? was a losing move. The rest of the game went **32 ♗f6 ♘c1+ 33 ♖xc1 ♕xf6 34 ♘b6 ♕b2+ 35 ♔d1 ♖f8 36 ♕e2 ♕d4+ 37 ♔e1 ♕g1+ 38 ♔d2 ♕d4+ 39 ♔e1 ♕xb6 40 ♕xe4+ ♔h8 41 ♖c2 d5 42 resigns**.

20. (a) Tal either bluffed or blundered. He could have resigned after 50...♕xh4!, e.g. 51 ♘d5 ♕d8!.

(b) Better was 50 ♘d5!. After 50...♕d6 51 ♘xb6! ♕xb6 52 ♘e5! he would have chances of saving the 52...♕c7 53 ♕xd7+ ♕xd7 54 ♘xd7 endgame.

After **50 ♘h4??** Black played **50...♕c7** and White failed to play 51 ♕xc7 and 52 ♘xg6 but he swindled Black later.

21. Both 45...♕e1 and 45...♕e2 would draw after 46 ♘xb7 ♕xf2+ 47 ♔h1 ♕f3+.

But **45...♕e2**, unlike the other move, did not threaten ...♕h1 mate. That induced White's second blunder, **46 ♕f8??**. He wanted to win with 47 ♕f7.

But he allowed 44...♗f3!. There was no perpetual check, so to avoid ...♕xf2 mate, White played **47 ♕f7+ ♔b8 48 ♕g8+ ♔c7 49 ♘e8+ ♔c6 50 ♕g6+ ♔b5 51 ♕b1+**.

After **51...♔a4 52 ♔g1 ♕xe8 53 ♕a2+ ♔b5 54 c4+ ♔c6 55 ♕a4+ b5** he eventually had to resign. The first blunder cost White $2,500 but the second one cost him more than $8,000.

22. (a) 34...♖d5 comes close, e.g. 35 ♗xd5 ♖d2 threatens 36...♗f4+ and mates. White has the edge if he gives his queen up, 36 ♕c4 ♗f4+ 37 ♕xf4 exf4+ 38 ♔xf4 ♗xd5 39 b7 ♗xb7 40 ♖xb7+. Better was 36...♗xd5.

(b) 35...♖dd2 fails to 36 ♕xe5+! ♔xe5 37 b8(♕)+. But 35...♖fd2! saves Black after 36 b8(♕) ♖xb8 37 ♕xb8 ♗f2+ 38 ♔g2 ♗a7+.

(c) Black wins after 36...g5!.

23. 21...g5~. White would still be in control after 22 ♘d4 and 22...gxf4 23 ♖xf4 because 23...♗h6 24 ♖df1! is a strong sacrifice.

Black would be lost after 24...♗xf4 25 ♖xf4 ♕d8 26 ♖g4+ ♔h8 27 ♕h6 or 25...♕h5 26 ♖f5. He would be close to it after 25...♕e7 26 ♘f5 ♕f8 27 ♕g3+ ♔h8 28 ♘d6.

Better is 23...♕g5 and 24 ♕f2 ♕xe5 25 ♖xf7 with survival chances.

But Black guessed right that one mistake (21 ♕e3?) would lead to others. White's advantage was gone after **22 ♘d5? gxf4 23 ♖xf4 ♕g5** because the e-pawn is falling. *(diagram)*

Play went **24 ♘f6+ ♔h8 "25 ♕f2 ♖xe5 26 ♘d4? ♗xf6 27 ♖xf6 ♗xg2** and Black fell apart, **28 ♔h2 ♖e3 29 ♕xg2 ♕xf6 30 ♕xb7 ♕f4+ White resigns.**

White's last chance for equality was 26 ♘g3. Kasparov said this was the last time he cried over a chess game.

24. 22...♖d1+! 23 ♖xd1 ♕a7 ended the attack and kept an extra knight.

25. 29 ♘xe6~ only works in two variations but it was the best try in a lost position.

Black saw one of them, 29...fxe6?? 30 ♕xg6+ and mates. He believed it was the only point of White's move. But that was a false narrative. He played **29...♕xe2??** and the game ended with **30 ♕xg6+! fxg6 31 f7+ ♔h7 32 ♖h3+ ♗h6 33 ♘g5+ ♔g7 34 ♘e6+ ♔h7 35 ♘g5+ draw.**

26. (a) No, **54...♖xg3+!** and **55 ♔xg3 ♕e5+!** since 56 ♕xe5 is stalemate.

(b) It is perpetual check after 55...♖xg3+ 56 ♔xg3 ♕g1+ 57 ♔f4 ♕c1+ and a book draw after 57 ♔h3 ♕e3+ 58 ♔g2 ♕xc5.

27. 55...♖xh5! because 56 ♖a5+ ♔b4 57 ♖xh5 is stalemate.

28. White threatens 38 ♖h8+ ♔e7 39 ♖h7 and 40 ♖xg7+ Then Black should draw with 39...♔f8 40 ♖h8+ ♔e7 41 ♖h7 ♔f8.

With **37...♖b4** he could meet 38 ♖h8+ ♔e7 39 ♖h7 with 39...♖xd4! 40 ♖xg7+ ♔d8.

But 37...♖b4 allowed **38 ♖h8+ ♔e7 39 ♗xf6+!** and draws after 39...gxf6 40 ♖h7+ ♔d8 41 ♖d7+ ♔c8 42 ♖e7+ ♔d8. Black tried **39...♔xf6 40 ♖xe8 ♖xb2** but agreed to a draw soon after **41 ♖f8+ ♔e5 42 ♖f7**.

29. 19...♕e6~ *(diagram)*

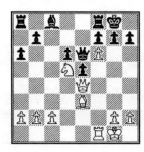

Then 20 ♘c7? ♕g4! is about equal and so is 20 ♖f5 ♕xd5.

This requires White to work a bit to win after 20 h3 g6 21 ♘c7 ♕xa2 28 ♘xa8 ♗f5.

Best, but harder to find, is 20 ♕h4 (threat of 21 ♕g5 g6 22 ♕h6) ♖e8 and then 21 h3!.

In the game, **20 ♖f3 ♖e8!** (not 20...♗d7 21 ♖h3) would have won after 21 h3.

But the game turned around with **21 ♖h3 ♕f5! 22 ♘e7+ ♖xe7 23 fxe7 ♗d7 24 ♕xb7 ♖e8 25 ♖f3 ♕e6 26 ♕xa6 f5 27 ♗f2? e4!** and Black eventually won.